WARSHIPS

From the Galley to the Present Day

George Grant
Angus Konstam
Leo Marriott

PRC

This edition first published in 2001 by
PRC Publishing Ltd,
Kiln House, 210 New Kings Road,
London SW6 4NZ

© 2001 PRC Publishing Ltd

ISBN 1 85648 600 1

Printed and bound in China

Contents

Introduction

During the course of recorded history, mankind has continually looked towards the sea as a provider of nourishment, as a channel for trade and for the migration of people or ideas. The last three millennia have witnessed the development of maritime craft from simple dugout through oared rafts, sailing ships, steam-powered ships to the fully-computerized supertankers and bulk cargo vessels of today. Throughout all this time, these maritime craft have fallen prey to the vagaries of weather, and to the hostile actions of other mariners. To defend them, specialized warships were developed, whose role of protection was only a part of their remit. Since the first known warships were commissioned by the rulers of Ancient Egypt, these craft have defended national interests and commerce, struggled for control of the seas with rival fleets of warships, and unleashed attacks against the shipping and coastline of enemy states. Warships have been instruments of both good and evil, and have influenced the course of humanity like no other man-made instrument in history. As arbiters of political destiny, military success and economic development, they hold a

unique place in our study of the past. At virtually any period in history from the dawn of the ancient world until the present day, warships have provided an accurate mirror of the technology of the civilization that produced them. For centuries, the wooden sailing ship represented the most advanced technological machine of its age and both before and since, warships have often led the way in the adoption of new maritime technology and design. Put simply, the warship represents one of the greatest technical achievements of its time. Evidence supplied by the study of warships through historical records, underwater archaeology and pictorial sources has helped us understand the technical limitations of the societies who produced these warships.

The story of the development of the warship is not purely a linear catalog of technical achievement. Instead, it represents a study of mankind's ability to improvise, adapt and to learn from past mistakes. Warships were produced to participate in naval warfare, and therefore elements of the nature of this conflict can be traced in their design, employment and ultimate fate. At the start of this book, naval warfare was essentially confined to the waters of the Mediterranean Sea, the cradle of numerous ancient civilizations. Following the emergence of the Roman Empire, the employment of warships can be traced to increasingly distant regions of the Roman world, and by the early modern period (also known as the Dark Ages), war at sea was a pan-European phenomenon. From the golden age of exploration during the late 15th and early 16th centuries, naval combat began to take place in the waters of the New

The quarterdeck of HMS _Queen Mary_. _Bison Picture Library_

World, as rival European powers vied for supremacy in the American continent and the waters that surrounded it. By the mid-18th century, warfare had become something which could cover the entire globe. By the 20th century, naval warfare fought on a global scale became the accepted norm. A knowledge of naval warfare, and of the warships which participated in it is vital if we are to understand why and how these conflicts helped shape the course of history.

During the course of history, certain ship types appeared which changed the course of naval warfare. These usually took place at a time of technological change, giving the creators of the new warship a brief superiority over their maritime rivals. These key groups of vessels include the triremes of Ancient Greece, the cog of the medieval world, the sailing ship-of-the-line, the ironclad, the dreadnought, the aircraft carrier and numerous others. All represented a leap which forced the world's navies to redefine themselves, often prompting an army race between these maritime powers.

Any historical study represents the conceptions of the historians who wrote it, as the analysis of historical information is often subjective. This is particularly noticeable when the work involves the study of technological innovation, and the development of the warship represents the ultimate in this field. Fortunately, in recent years more sources are available to the historian that ever before. Recent discoveries in underwater archaeology, and the release of previously unavailable information have allowed us to re-examine our understanding of warship development. This work contains a historical appraisal of warship development, and incorporates this latest information. It also presents a complex subject in a fresh and accessible way.

To achieve this, the publishers have drawn together several leading maritime and naval historians, and collectively their analysis of the subject sheds new light on the warship, its evolution and employment. All of these authors have demonstrated a lifelong passion for naval history, and their enthusiasm seeps through the pages of this study. The work traces the development of the warship from earliest times, through its use in the ancient and medieval world to the golden age of the sailing warship. From there, it traces a series of technological innovations that spurred on the ever-increasing rate of warship evolution, and the supremacy of a succession of warship types. The advent of the ironclad to the launch of a nuclear-powered aircraft carrier spanned only a century in historical terms, but covered one of the most dynamic periods of technological change in mankind's history.

The one lesson we can learn from a study of the development of the warship is that revolutions in naval warfare can rarely be predicted. The nation with a technological edge and the largest industrial capacity will best be able to win a naval arms race. As the same was true for ancient Greece, 19th century Britain or 21st century America, this ability is closely allied to the creation and maintenance of seapower; the ability to protect and maintain control of the sea lanes. Naval analysts trying to determine future developments might do worse than examining the entire sweep of naval history encompassed by this book. Above all, this study bears witness to the struggle of mariners and shipbuilders to overcome the limitations imposed upon them.

ABOVE LEFT: **Built by Thornycroft, HMS *Amazon* was launched in 1926 and the design formed the basis of all British destroyer construction almost up to the outbreak of war in 1939.**
via Leo Marriott

ABOVE: **The USS *Tinosa* was one of the war standard "Gato" class and was completed in early 1943. She is shown returning to Pearl Harbor after a successful war patrol in 1944. Note the small Japanese flags flying from the gun and periscope standards denoting ships or aircraft claimed as destroyed.**
Bison Picture Library

RIGHT: **The successors to the "Daring" class were the "County" class guided missile destroyers, which were built during the 1960s. Although still carrying a powerful gun battery, the main armament was the Seaslug medium-range SAM which was fired from a launcher on the stern. The substantial bulk of these ships was due to the volume of the missile magazines. A Wessex ASW helicopter was also embarked. D12 is HMS *Kent*, launched in 1961. She displaced 6,200 tons.**
via L.Marriott

The Ancient World
RAMS AND RAIDERS

Recent archaeological finds from Scotland and Holland suggest that carved-out wooden dugouts were used by Mesolithic mariners around 6000BC. These dugouts eventually developed into larger and more seaworthy vessels, powered by wind and sail. The first evidence for shipping in the Mediterranean comes from ancient Egypt, where a depiction of a sailing vessel on a decorative vase has been dated to 3200BC. This simple papyrus-reed boat was purely a river craft, designed for use on the Nile, but within five centuries far more complex vessels were being produced. The wooden "Cheops" boat was discovered in the Great Pyramid and dates from 2600BC. Although wooden, its design resembled earlier papyrus vessels. It would take another thousand years for dedicated warships to emerge, although enigmatic Minoan illustrations from 2800BC may depict vessels fitted with a ram. Bas-reliefs in the burial chamber of Queen Hatshepsut from 1500BC depict seagoing vessels, with keels, frames and crossbeams. Hawsers stretched from stem to stern provided extra strength for

ABOVE: **A Roman mosaic depicting two galleons.** © *CORBIS*

BELOW: **A terracotta model of a Hellenistic warship from Erment in Egypt, dating to the end of the 4th century BC.** *Nationalmuseet Copenhagen, via TRH Pictures*

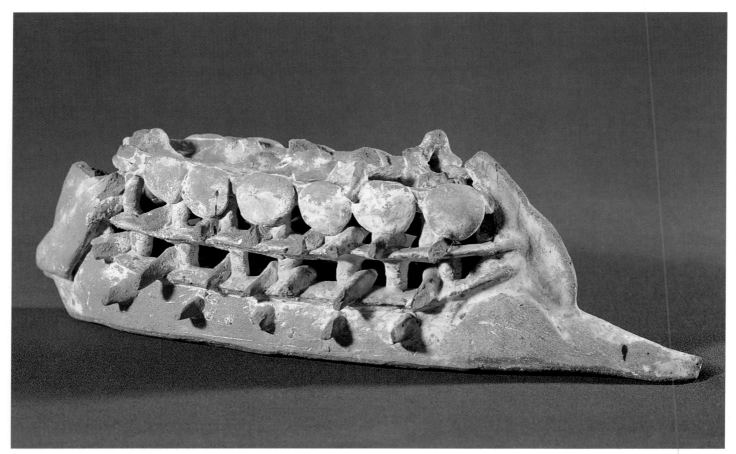

these vessels. These ships were propeled by both oars and sails, but they were clearly merchant vessels, not warships.

Around 1200BC the "Sea Peoples" threatened to invade Egypt. These intruders came from the northern Mediterranean, and probably included the Cretans and Philistines. The Pharaoh Ramses III defeated them, and celebrated his victory by constructing a temple. It was decorated with scenes depicting a naval battle, the first such representation in recorded history. His Egyptian fleet consisted of specially-designed warships, resembling earlier Egyptian craft but slimmer, and fitted with rams and fighting positions. A single mast with a square sail carried a wicker fighting platform. Between six and eleven oars were used on these craft, while the craft of the "Sea Peoples" were similar, but they lacked oars. Evidence suggests that by the 12th century BC, both Egypt and Babylon had powerful navies, charged with protecting shipping from pirate attacks and for use in time of war. The main combat power of these warships came from archers, indicating that missile fire and ramming were favored over hand-to-hand clashes.

The single bank of oars on Egyptian warships of this period limited the effectiveness of these earliest warships, and in later centuries naval designers sought to increase propulsive power by adding further tiers of oarsmen. In time, two or more tiers of oarsmen were added, and warships came to be classified by the number of oar banks they carried. The Greek, Phoenecian and Assyrian war galleys of the tenth to the eighth centuries BC were significantly more powerful than the craft which preceded them, mainly due to

their use of a second tier of oars, creating the "bireme." Representations of Aegean warships on ceramics showed vessels equipped with a ram, with an outrigger attached to the main hull to protect the oars. Biremes were warships with two tiers of oars, and the first unequivocal depiction of one dates from the eighth century BC. There is an Assyrian relief that represents a Phoenecian warship, with a slim, solid wooden lower hull, with two banks of oars, the upper ones sitting inboard of the others. An upper "bridge" or "fighting deck" provided a platform for archers or spearmen. Both the Greek and Assyrian (or Phoenecian) warships were fitted with a large ram, sheathed in metal (bronze). Unlike earlier warships, these craft could perform no other function, being poorly designed to carry provisions or cargo. These were purely instruments of naval power.

From the sixth century BC pictures of Greek warships on ceramic finds show another evolution in Mediterranean ship design. These vessels were lighter than the Doric Greek or Phoenecian craft of previous centuries, with elegant lines and an improved layout of oars and rowers. Light ribbed frames supported two oar banks on either side of the craft, separated by a central walkway. This central walkway also provided reinforcement to the hull, rather like the

BELOW: **Detail of a Roman mosaic from Palazzo Barberini at Palestrina, dating from the 1st century BC. It is similar to warships depicted in similar mosaics in Pompei.**
©*Archivo Iconografico, S.A./CORBIS*

ABOVE: **Carving from the acropolis of Lindos on Rhodes showing the typical tall plumed sterns and inwardly curving sterns which were characteristic of Roman warships dating from the 1st century AD.**
©*Wolfgang Kaehler/CORBIS*

LEFT: **Ulysses and the Sirens, a 3rd century AD mosaic from the House of Ulysses and Dionysius at Dougga, in Tunisia. This stylized Roman bireme shows the sail arrangement used by Roman warships of this period.**
©*Charles & Josette Lenars/CORBIS*

stretched rope found in earlier Egyptian craft. These vessels also had a pronounced keel, ending in a curved stern and vertical stem-post, which was also fitted with a ram. It has been suggested that the ram was only loosely attached to the vessel itself, so that if it was torn loose or damaged, the structural integrity of the ship would not be threatened. While outriggers were still used, some depictions show that the lower bank of oars passed through holes cut in the side of the hull, and the upper bank rested on the rail of the vessel.

In Homer's *Illiad*, the "Black Ships of Troy" were Greek bireme galleys of this type, with 50 oars per vessel. These "pentaconters" had two banks of 12 oars per side, plus two steering oars in the stern. Lighter versions fitted with 30 oars ("triaconters") were also mentioned, and were probably used as pirate-hunters, raiders and as scouting vessels. The largest of these biremes were probably under 80ft long, which meant they carried a crew of less than 100

FAR RIGHT: **The bireme was a sensible way to increase power without the problems associated with increased length. This example is called a "hemiola," or "one-and-a-half," because the rear 14 rowers acted as deck hands and could therefore man sail while the ship was still under oars.** *Chrysalis Images*

RIGHT AND BELOW: **The 50-oared vessels to which Homer refers could either have been biremes or, as illustrated here, a galley with one bank of 25 oars on each side.** *Chrysalis Images*

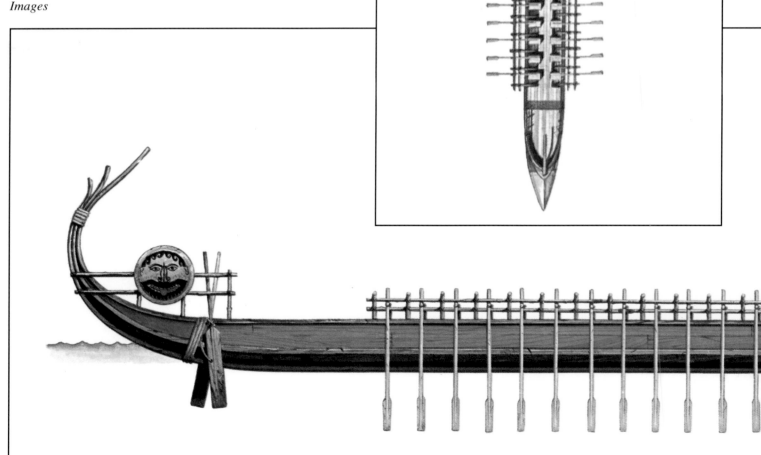

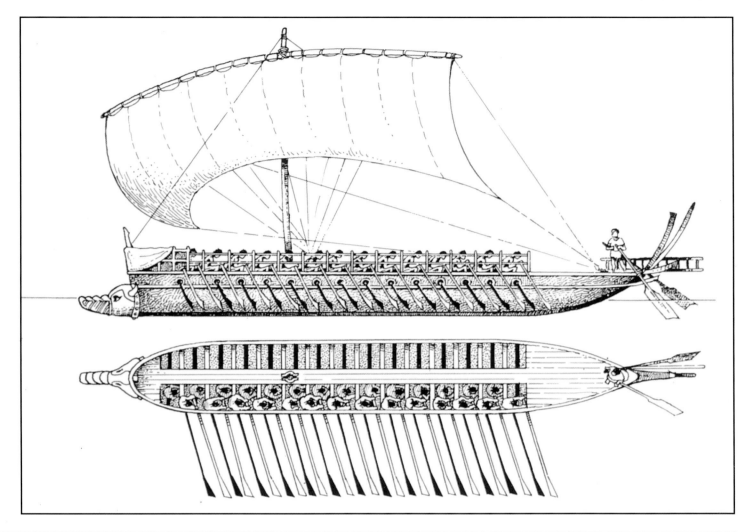

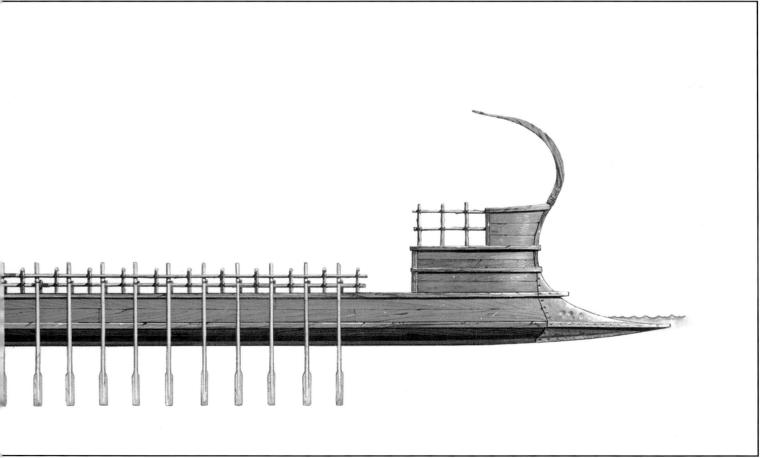

men. Little is known about the early development of these specialist warships, and how they turned into the triremes of the fifth century BC. Thucydides, born in 471BC, recorded that triremes were first developed by Corinthian shipwrights during the seventh century BC. Amenocc the shipbuilder was credited with the invention, but other evidence supports a Phoenecian origin. Certainly, both biremes and early triremes existed at the same time during the era which saw the development of the Greek city states, and the assimilation of the Phoenecians into the Persian Empire.

The trireme is the most widely known warship of the ancient world, a symbol of Greek power and influence. These oared warships were characterized by the organization of their oarsmen into three rowing tiers. Evidence for these vessels comes from a handful of Greek writers, as well as from artistic representations. Many of these confuse rather than reinforce our understanding of the trireme. Intense academic debate raged over the layout of a trireme's oar banks, but the construction of a full-scale replica vessel by the Greek government has provided a unique source of practical evidence. The *Olympias* is an

BELOW AND RIGHT: **Greek trireme c500BC. This 170-man vessel would not have ventured far from shore due to its instability and the need to beach for supplies.** *Chrysalis Images*

FAR RIGHT: **The *Diekplus* tactic involved a line-ahead attack by a faster fleet. The lead vessel would sheer of the oars of the enemy, leave it to be finished off by the next boat and head for a new target.** *Chrysalis Images*

The Trireme

The trireme, with its triple bank of oars, was developed in the fifth century BC as a natural successor to the bireme used by the Phoenicians. These first oar-propeled narrow-beamed warships were much more maneuverable than the cumbersome merchant sailing ships which had hitherto also been used for fighting. The trireme, which could reach speeds of up to 9kt, was built with a reinforced prow below the waterline, enabling it to ram its enemy, holing its hull and shattering its oars as well as being able to grapple and board an enemy with its soldiers, using archers to fire on the enemy. The cost of constructing and maintaining a fleet of triremes and their large crews was high, and only the wealthiest states could afford to do so. The basis of the Athenian empire's military strength was its sea power. A fleet of up to 300 triremes was maintained, allowing its steersmen and oarsmen to become highly proficient, turning the trireme ram into an extremely effective weapon when matched against less experienced crews which relied solely on boarding. The difficulty of replacing trained steersmen and oarsmen was shown when Athens was forced to sue for peace to end the Peloponnesian War after its fleet was massacred by the Spartans at the Battle of Aegospotami in 404BC. Although triremes did have a square sail, sea battles tended to be fought close to land as the large crews of around 200 men and the intensive labor involved in rowing the triremes meant that they would have provisions for only a few days at sea. By the fourth and third centuries BC, the trireme was being superseded by even more powerful warships, the quadriremes and quinquiremes (four and five banks of oars) developed by the Romans and Carthaginians.

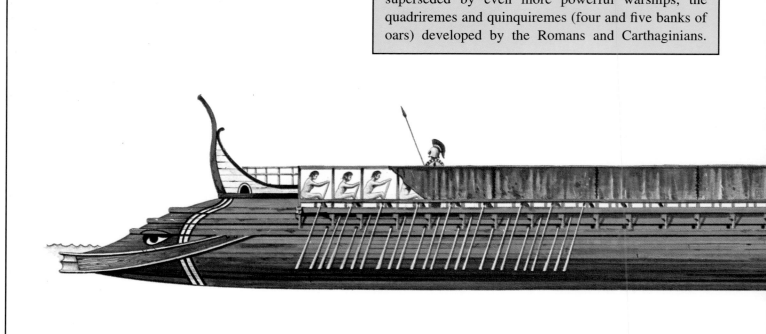

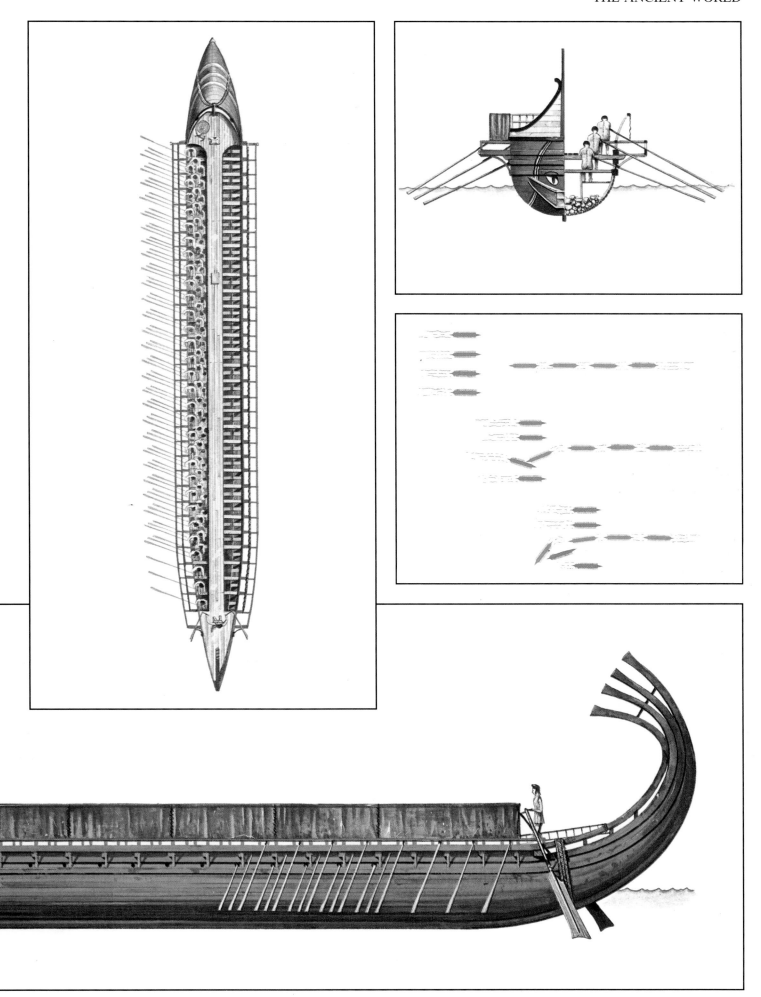

accurate reconstruction of an Athenian trireme of the fifth and fourth centuries BC based on the latest research. Designed by naval architect John Coates, she was commissioned into the Greek Navy in 1987.

Like the original triremes, the *Olympias* was powered by 170 oarsmen, in three tiers, each higher and closer to the vessel's centerline than the last. The "thranites" were on top, the "zygians" (or zygites) in the center, and the "thalamians" (or thalamites) on the bottom. The oars varied in length, with those in the lowest tier being the shortest. It was steered by two stern side rudders, and a single mast carried a square sail to augment the propulsion supplied by the oars. Two sails were usually carried, of different weights, and in some early (pre-4th century BC) examples, a small second mast was mounted nearer the bow, carrying a foresail. These masts were lowered before the triremes went into battle, so propulsion in combat was exclusively provided by oarsmen.

The principal weapon of the trireme was its ram, an extension of the keel beam. In battle, they would increase speed at a constant rate, reaching a maximum speed just before contact with the enemy. The ram would batter into the hull of an enemy warship, piercing the hull. Even a glancing blow could damage oars on the enemy vessel, rendering her defenseless. A central walkway and bow and stern platforms provided space for marines. The top speed

ABOVE: **Detail of the Lenormant relief dating from around 400 BC, showing the open framework at the top level. A leather screen — the parablemata — was hung from this to protect the rowers against missiles.** ©*Gianni Dagli Orti/CORBIS*

of the reconstructed trireme *Olympias* has been logged at 10 knots. A common misconception was that galleys were powered by slaves. In Ancient Greece, oarsmen were freemen, and only the fittest and strongest were selected for service. The trireme commander — the Trierach — controlled the operation of the ship in action. He was assisted by the Hortator, whose task was to encourage these oarsmen and to extort them to greater efforts. The big advantage the Greeks had over their rivals was that their oarsmen were Greek citizens, not slaves. Their future and that of their home state was directly influenced by their efforts at the oars. These Greek oarsmen and the galleys they rowed faced their greatest challenge at the Battle of Salamis (480 BC). In what was probably the most significant naval battle to take place in the ancient world, the Greeks defeated a numerically superior Persian force through tactical skill and strategic cunning. Technically, their triremes were also superior to those of the enemy, and their crews had a better morale, being free men and not slaves.

During the fourth century BC, the shipbuilders in the Greek colony of Syracuse in Sicily experimented with

Battle of Salamis

In 480BC the Persians led by Xerxes invaded the Greek city states. The resources of the Persian empire were vast in comparison to that of the Greeks and the Persian army advanced towards Athens, which had been abandoned by its populace. Under the command of Themistocles, the allied Greek fleet, manned by many of the refugees, laid in wait off Athens in the straits between Attica and the island of Salamis for the Persian fleet following its army. The Persian fleet was numerically superior (an estimated 1,200 ships against 368 Greek ships) but the Greek triremes had the advantage of having taller decks and being more strongly constructed. After waiting for the Greeks to emerge from the straits the Persian fleet entered the narrow waters in late September 480BC. The battle lasted all day, the entire Persian fleet being bottled up and finding it difficult to maneuver, enabling the heavier Greek triremes to target their opponents, ramming and sinking 200 of the increasingly panicked Persian ships for the loss of only 40 Greek ships. For Xerxes, watching the battle from his throne on a nearby headland, it was the end of the Persian fleet as an effective fighting force and of his dream of conquering Greece.

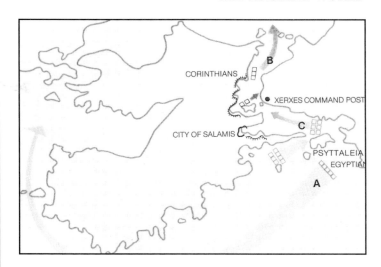

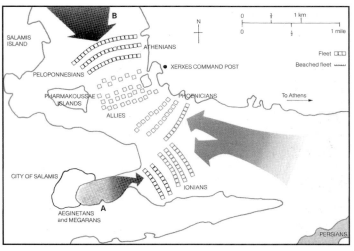

TOP AND ABOVE: **The battle of Salamis 480BC. The first stage sees the Greeks set a trap for Xerxes, first by feeding false information that led him to send his Egyptian vessels (A) to block the Megarian channel, then by luring the larger Persian fleet into confined waters by a false retreat (B). Xerxes fell into the trap, is ambushed by the Aeginetans and Megarans and then cut to pieces by the numerically inferior Athenian fleet.** *Chrysalis Images*

LEFT: **A highly fanciful image of the battle of Salamis. The unfurled sails and triple-tiered ram are particularly erroneous — galleys went into battle with sails and masts packed away.** *©Bettmann/CORBIS*

ABOVE: **Another Victorian view of the naval battles of the ancient world — the Athenians are beaten in Syracuse harbor.** ©*Bettmann/CORBIS*

BELOW AND RIGHT: **A Septireme — the most likely answer to the riddle of galley development is that the banks of involved numbers of rowers on the same oar as shown (top right).** *Chrysalis Images*

Siege of Syracuse

The Peloponnesian War (431BC-404BC) was fought between the two power blocs of Athens and Sparta, and their allies. During the war the maritime city state of Syracuse on Sicily presented an attractive target to Athenian imperial ambitions, both because of its wealth and its large navy, which was a challenge to Athenian maritime supremacy. Led by Alcibiades, the Athenians poured enormous resources into two massive invasion fleets which were sent to win Sicily, over 800 miles from Athens, in a campaign which lasted two years (415BC-413BC). The Athenian and allied army totalled 40,000, of which nearly virtually all perished or were enslaved in the campaign. The Athenian attempt to starve Syracuse into surrender by a siege failed when a Syracusan force broke through Athenian lines in 413BC. The Athenian fleet in Syracuse's large harbor was then also trapped by the Syracusans, assisted by a resurgant Spartan fleet led by the Spartan general Gylippus, and annihilated, the Athenians and their allies losing 116 triremes. The Athenian land forces were left cut off and forced to surrender after suffering huge losses in series of attacks led by the formidable Syracusan cavalry. Athens never recovered from the destruction of its fleet and army, which left it undefended at home, and in 404BC was forced to sue for peace with Sparta.

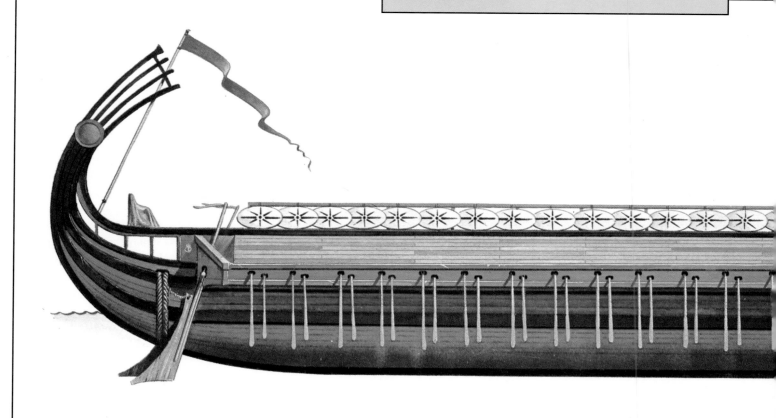

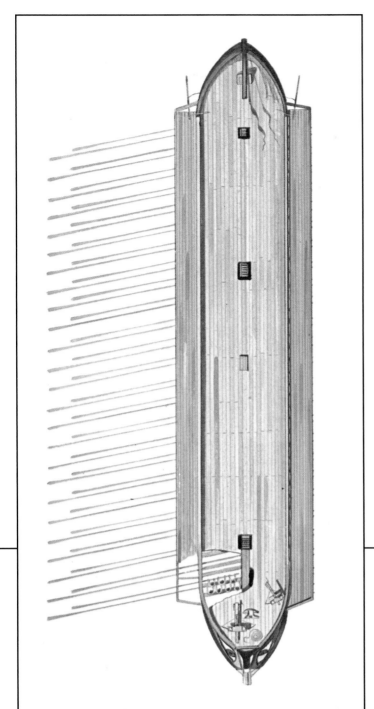

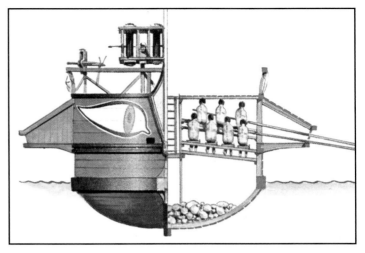

"quadriremes" and "quinquiremes", which historians always imagined were galleys with four or five banks of oars. Experiments with the reconstructed trireme have shown that technically, three banks of oars is the maximum which can be employed without risk of the oars fouling each other. It is now considered more likely that these were large triremes, with four or five men at each oar. Some classical references describe galleys with fifteen or more banks, but once again, this is misleading. These higher numbers represent multiples of oarsmen assigned to each oar, the largest being associated with Imperial Roman pleasure barges rather than warships. Clearly, the larger the number of oarsmen, the longer the oar had to be inside the vessel, and the further it moved. Consequently, the inboard oarsmen needed to race to keep up with the sweep if the oars,

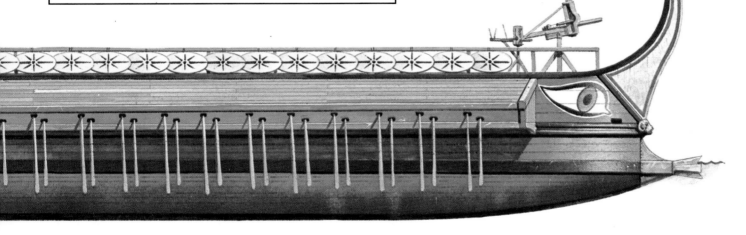

Julius Caesar and Mark Anthony

Julius Caesar (c100-44BC) rose to power following a series of successful military campaigns to extend the Roman empire culminating in the Gallic wars (58-52BC) in which he conquered all of Gaul (France) as well today's Belgium and parts of the Netherlands and Germany. Caesar's military genius and the superior might of the Roman army was effectively demonstrated in these wars but naval power was also significant. The Roman warship by then had developed into a large fighting machine and Caesar built a fleet of biremes to control the coast of Gaul, using his ships to grapple and board the lighter ships of the Veneti opposing him, on which his legionnaries could then overwhelm the crew. Control of the seas enabled him to launch two raids across the English Channel to Britain in 55 and 54BC, but although he used ship-borne mechanical artillery of catapults and ballistae to provide cover for the successful landings of his legions, he was unable to establish a base. Co-ruler of Rome from 61BC with Pompey and Crassus, Caesar seized power after he and his legions crossed the River Rubicon in 49BC to enter Italy. He defeated Pompey the same year, but increasing disquiet about his authoritarian rule at home led to his assassination in 44BC. Mark Anthony (c83-30BC), who had assisted Caesar on his campaigns, was left briefly in power following Caesar's death, but then shared power in a triumvirate with Octavian and Lepidus from 43BC to 32BC. However, Anthony and Octavian's rivalry led to the breakdown of the triumvirate and in the ensuing civil war, Anthony was defeated at the naval battle of Actium in 31BC by Octavian's admiral Agrippa, the battle being notable for Agrippa's use of light, maneuverable biremes, known as Liburnian galleys, to counter Anthony's larger ships. These more agile ships were later to gradually supersede the massive Roman triremes and quinquiremes. Anthony fled the battle to rejoin his ally and lover Cleopatra in Egypt, and both committed suicide the next year.

while the outboard oarsman hardly needed to move at all. The Romans and Persians both employed the same basic trireme design as the Greeks, but their vessels were identifiable by certain regional variations. For example, the Phoenecians, serving the Persian Empire, designed triremes with higher sterns than their Greek counterparts, as accounts of the battle of Salamis describe them being caught by the wind, making them hard to steer. For their part, the Carthaginians and, later, the Romans relied on the larger and more complex quinquireme design. Roman bas-reliefs and mosaics depict Greek, Roman and Carthaginian galleys from the fourth century BC onward.

While the Greek city states became embroiled in a destructive war between Athens and Sparta which would last three decades, new maritime powers were rising in the west. The city of Carthage developed a powerful navy during the third century BC, and when she became embroiled in a conflict with Republican Rome in 264BC, she maintained an unrivaled naval supremacy in the Western Mediterranean. The base of the Statue of Winged Victory from Samothrace, dating from the fourth century BC shows what these Carthaginian warships might have looked like. Now in the Louvre in Paris, the statue shows the bows of

RIGHT: **Caesar crossing the English Channel on his 55BC raid. As is typical of many 18th century renditions, this image has little to recommend it to the historian, particularly the massive crenellated castle in the background.** ©*Bettmann/CORBIS*

galleys, almost cerainly biremes. A Roman bas-relief in Rhodes shows the stern of the same type of vessel, and dates from the third century BC. These vessels have a boxed-in outrigger (known to the Greeks as a "parados"). The three tiers of oars are shown protruding from below, the center of and the top of this gunwale. A Roman warship shown on a bas-relief from Praeneste dating from the early second century BC shows that this "parados" has been converted into a walkway for marines, extending the space available for soldiers on the vessel.

We know that Republican Roman warships were copied from those used by the Carthaginians, so we can assume that both Roman and Carthaginian warships were similar in appearance and design. At first the Romans had relied on the naval power of their allies, such as Syracuse in Sicily, but these craft were probably triremes which followed the traditional Greek model. The Carthaginians had developed working quinquiremes, giving them a larger platform for soldiers, and a greater ramming power. When a quinquireme was wrecked on the coast of Sicily, its construction methods were copied and then Roman shipwrights were ordered to produce 100 similar warships. The Roman navy was born.

Under the leadership of the Consul Caius Duilius the Roman navy emerged triumphant over their Carthaginian rivals during the Punic Wars. Unlike the Greeks and Carthaginians who emphasized ramming tactics, the Romans relied on their trained citizen soldiers to carry the day. The two tactical innovations which helped win the naval war for Rome were the grappling hook and the "corvus." Grappling hooks were used to snare a nearby galley and bring the two ships alongside each other. The "corvus" was a wooden gangway which could be lowered, creating a secure bridge from one ship to the other. Once the marines gained a foothold on the enemy vessel, the battle was virtually over, as the Carthaginian crews were smaller and less well-trained. Unable to match Roman manpower and resources, and finding themselves at a tactical disadvantage, the Carthaginian navy proved no match for the Romans. The same basic quinquireme variant of the older trireme design remained in use until the end of the Roman Republic, when a lack of maritime opponents in the Mediterranean removed the need for a powerful navy. The last great trial for the design came during the battles of the Roman Civil War between Caesar and Pompey, and then between Octavian and Mark Anthony. The Battle of Actium pitted a Romano-Egyptian fleet led by Mark Anthony against a Roman fleet commanded by Octavian. As was the case during the Punic Wars, the battle was fought as a series of boarding actions, where the training of Octavian's marines proved superior to those of Anthony and Cleopatra.

Following the end of the Punic Wars, with the exception of the Civil War and its aftermath, the Mediterranean became a Roman lake. The only serious maritime threat to the "Pax Romana" came from pirates rather than from rival

Pompey

Rome in the first century BC was continually wracked by civil conflict led by powerful military leaders. Pompey the Great (106-48BC) was an outstanding general and his victories in Sicily and Africa enabled Rome to assert its control over territories abroad. At home, he put down the slave uprising led by Spartacus (71BC) and was elected consul in 70BC. Rome was then threatened by pirates, allied with Mithridates VI, cutting off its food supplies in the Mediterranean. In 67BC Pompey was given powers to commission a fleet of up to 270 warships and an army of 125,000 men to defeat the pirates. In three months the pirate threat was eliminated by Pompey's systematic cleansing of the Mediterranean, and Mithridates was defeated the following year. Thereafter, Rome recognized the need for maritime power and established the beginnings of a permanent fleet.

After this, Pompey was given control of Rome's eastern empire, where he set up an efficient administration. At the height of his power, he returned to Italy and with Julius Caesar and Crassus assumed power as the first triumvirate in 61BC. In 55BC Pompey became proconsul of Spain, but by then he was vying with Caesar for power in Italy. As Caesar crossed the Rubicon from his province of Gaul to enter Italy in 49BC, Pompey took his fleet across the Adriatic to Dyrrhachium (Dubrovnik). He was hoping to use his dominance of the seas to blockade Caesar in Italy, but although his fleet numbered up to 600 ships and Caesar could raise only 150 vessels, he failed to prevent Caesar following him with his army across the Adriatic. Despite having the larger army, Pompey was defeated by Caesar in 48BC at the Battle of Pharsalus, and was assassinated shortly after in Egypt.

ABOVE: **1820 etching of Caesar being shown the head of his rival Pompey. Pompey was instrumental in defeating piracy in the Mediterranean.** ©*Bettmann/CORBIS*

states. Finding the lumbering quinqueremes were unsuited to warfare against these pirates, Pompey returned to the simpler bireme design. These pirate-hunting vessels were powered by 88 oarsmen, with two to an oar. Fast and maneuverable, they also carried a contingent of Roman marines. Within a decade, piracy was virtually wiped out in the Mediterranean. For the next five centuries, the only warships required in the Roman world were small biremes which served in punitive or policing roles. Even the warships built by Caesar to invade Britain in 54BC were biremes rather than large warships.

Although galleys remained in use as warships throughout the ancient period and survived the fall of the Roman Empire, the heyday of galley warfare had passed. Merchant shipping was exclusively powered by sail, and following the barbarian invasions, only the Byzantines retained galleys as dedicated warships in Mediterranean waters. Despite this, the tradition of galley design survived, and the region would experience a revival in the use of the war galley a thousand years after the demise of the great galley fleets of the ancient world.

FAR RIGHT: **The battle of Actium, a wonderful Victorian image of the battle.** ©*Carmen Redondo/CORBIS*

BELOW: **Later Roman warships, the massive "Deceres,"**
with its fighting towers, catapults and grappling hooks.
Chrysalis Images

Battle of Actium

The naval battle of Actium in 31BC was the culminating event in the civil war between Octavian (later the Roman emperor Augustus) and his rival Mark Anthony. The defeat and subsequent suicide of Anthony left the way clear for Octavian to take over the Roman republic as Emperor Augustus. The battle was fought off Acarnania on the northwest coast of Greece. Mark Anthony, in alliance with Queen Cleopatra of Egypt, had drawn up his fleet of 500 ships in a strait, with his 70,000-strong army encamped nearby on land. Octavian, meanwhile, used his own army of 80,000 infantry to block Anthony's access to the south, while his fleet blockaded Anthony to the north. Dwindling supplies forced Anthony's hand and he brought his fleet out of the bay on 2 September 31BC. Octavian's fleet, under the command of Marcus Vipsanius Agrippa, attacked in a crescent formation, intending to outflank Anthony. For much of the day the engagement was inconclusive, attacks being carried out by ramming, firing missiles (sometimes burning) into opposing ships or close-quarter fighting — Anthony's squadron of 220 larger ships with stone-throwing catapults being nullified by Octavian's smaller but more maneuverable ships. The battle was decided when Cleopatra fled with her squadron of 60 galleys. Anthony followed her with a few of his own ships, leaving the main part of his fleet behind. Disheartened by the loss of its commander, Anthony's fleet succumbed to Octavian's ships, his abandoned army surrendering a week later.

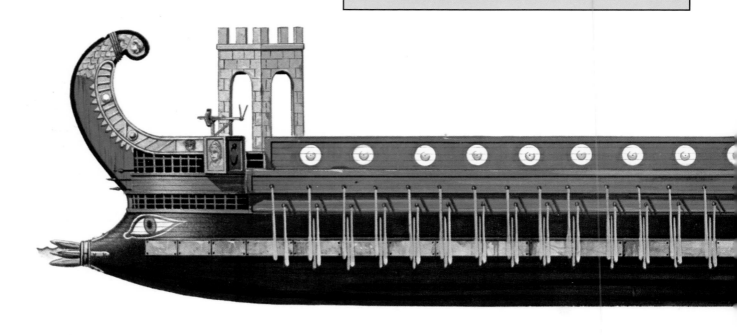

The Middle Ages
GREEK FIRE AND CANNON

From the late fourth century onward, the Western Roman Empire was submerged by successive waves of barbarian invaders. These peoples swept through Western Europe into Spain and Italy, leaving only the Eastern Empire intact. This surviving portion of the Roman world subsequently became known as the Byzantine Empire, and survived for another thousand years. In the west, all traces of a Roman navy were swept aside, and when they reached the Mediterranean these invaders relied on the indigenous forms of shipping they found there. In northern Europe, the barbarians raided the coasts of Britain and Gaul with their own peculiar vessels; long open boats powered by oar and

sail. The development of the great warships of the golden age of sail can be traced back to these barbarian raiding craft of the fifth century AD. The Romans in Britain and Gaul developed their own shipbuilding traditions, but there is no evidence to suggest that these vessels continued to be

ABOVE: **Relic from a Norwegian Vikingship.** *Hulton Getty Picture Collection*

BELOW: **Danish longboats defeated by Alfred the Great's navy near Swanage, Dorset; from a print by Colin Gill. Naval warfare at this time was simply hand-to-hand combat of the type practiced on land.** *Hulton Getty Picture Collection*

built much after the collapse of the Western Roman Empire. Instead, Scandinavian and Germanic forms of ship construction were copied throughout Northern Europe.

At Nydam in Denmark, the remains of raiding boats of this kind were discovered, dating from around 350AD. In 1939 the remains of a Anglo-Saxon vessel dating from around 600AD were found inside a burial mound at Sutton Hoo, in Suffolk. Both craft were oar-powered, and had no mast. These vessels were clinker-built, where outer planks were fastened to a series of frames rising from a keel. The edges of these outer planks overlapped each other. By contrast, in the Mediterranean, most ships were carvel-built, where the planks were joined edge to edge, using mortise and tenon joints. The tendency was also to build these southern European craft using "shell-first" construction, a method where strength was imparted by the outer hull itself, not by internal frames. By contrast the "frame-first" construction of Northern Europe produced a stronger but heavier vessel.

In 1920, the remains of two Norse ships were found at Kvalsund in Norway. Dating from around 700AD, these were broader than the earlier vessels, and may have carried a mast. The adoption of the sail in northern European vessels took place around the late seventh century AD. Decorated stones from this period were found on the Swedish island of Gotland which depicted vessels with single masts and square sails. During the eighth century, a shorter, rounder version of these vessels came into being. Known as the "knorr," this vessel was used to transport cargo, and it was primarily propeled by wind and sail. These knorrs plied the waters of the Baltic and North seas, or carried explorers to Greeenland and even North America. Although merchant ships, these craft evolved into a medieval vessel type that serve both as a warship and as a cargo carrier.

The knorrs were the most common vessels of the Viking age, and archaeological evidence suggests similar vessels were used in Carolingian France, Anglo-Saxon England and in Germany. Despite this evidence of widespread use, their role has been overshadowed by the Viking longship. These vessels were fighting ships, and varied in size, the smallest (and most prevalent) having 16-20 oars a side, each pulled by two oarsmen. Larger versions had 25, 30 or even 40 oars. The latter type of longship was known as a "draakar" or dragon ship, and normally served as the flagship for a Norse king or warlord. A wooden dragon's head was discovered in the Schelde estuary, and probably once served as the stem decoration on one of these dragon ships. These decorations were not carried on all longships, and they could be detached when not in use. These longships all shared certain characteristics. They were long, slim, elegant vessels, with double-skinned clinker-built hulls. Although powered by oars, they also carried a single mast, carrying a large square sail. Made using local cloth, it was reinforced

Alfred the Great

Alfred the Great (849-99AD), king of the West Saxon kingdom of Wessex from 871AD to his death, is known as the "father of the English navy." When he came to the throne, the Saxon kingdoms of England were under continual threat from the Danes, or Vikings. After he had pushed the Danes out of Wessex in the early years of his reign, he extended West Saxon influence and protection over the other Saxon kingdoms in England outside the Danelaw, the area north and east of London ceded to the Danes. He established effective defensive measures against future Danish attack by building and strengthening forts manned by his reorganized army and by rebuilding his fleet, which he stationed along the coast. He ordered new larger and faster 60-oar ships to be built from 875AD to enable him to engage the Danish longships at sea before they could land and his navy was effective in countering a large-scale Danish invasion led by King Haesten from continental Europe. Although Danish coastal raids continued after 896AD Alfred was secure in his control of Wessex, West Mercia and Kent, recapturing London and having prevented the fall of the whole of England into Danish hands. He is also remembered as an able administrator and a great scholar king.

ABOVE: **Alfred the Great.** *Hulton Getty Picture Collection*

by a pattern of diagonal stitching. The development of these longships coincided with an expansion by the Norsemen into Russia and Western Europe, and from 800AD these vessels carried Viking raiders as far south as the Mediterranean.

The well-preserved remains of ship burials from Southern Norway provide us with examples of these craft. The "Oseberg ship" dates from the ninth century AD, and was highly decorated, with a low freeboard; probably a royal pleasure craft than a warship. Historians have linked her with a vessel type known as a "karv," a form of coastal craft. Although not a true longship, her hull was built along the same lines as contemporary warships. The "Gokstad ship" was larger, and her clinker-built hull was pierced for 16 oars per side. It had a more powerful mast and a higher freeboard than the Oseberg ship, and was evidently capable of making long voyages — a replica of the craft made a successful Atlantic crossing in 28 days. The Gokstad vessel has been dated to the 10th century, and was probably a cross between a warship and a trading vessel. Norse sagas contain numerous accounts of longships being used in action. Longships were sometimes lashed together, creating large rafts, which served as fighting platforms. Although the Norsemen used archers, combat at sea involved hand-to-hand fighting, and the side with the best fighting platform had an advantage over their adversaries. Evidence from the sagas suggests that some longships had decked platforms at the bow and stern called "lyfting" which were used as fighting positions.

The Vikings

The Vikings were raiders, traders and settlers from Norway, Sweden and Denmark. Since the 790s the Danes had practiced fast, mobile warfare using their shallow-draught longships to raid coasts and inland waters, as well as move their armies fast inland, and by the mid-11th century had conquered and colonized large parts of Britain, Normandy and Russia, as well as reaching into the Mediterranean, across the Atlantic to North America and as far east as India. The Viking longship was extremely seaworthy and carried typically 60 warriors, who were also rowers, and even horses. Although the Vikings could fight at sea by grappling and boarding, the technological advantage held over other contemporary warships enabled them to raid at will and disappear before an effective force could be raised against them. The first major raids were on the monasteries of Lindisfarne and Jarrow on the Northumbrian coast of England in 793AD and 794AD respectively and by 840AD the Vikings had settled in Dublin and much of Ireland, and England north and east of London was also controlled under the Danelaw. Iceland was colonized from c900AD, with Eric the Red later settling Greenland and his son Leif Eriksson reaching North America. The coast of Frisia and northern France was also settled following a series of raids, the Viking chief Rollo reaching an agreement with the Franks to settle in the Seine valley — the origins of Normandy. For 300 years the Vikings were the dominant sea power in Europe but by the end of the 11th century the threat they posed the rest of Europe faded with the decline of Norway and Sweden, the separation of Denmark and the rise of powerful new blocs such as the Normans, ironically themselves originally Viking settlers.

ABOVE RIGHT: **The clinker-built frame construction is noticeable in this photograph of the remains of a small Norse** *velle* **recovered from Roskilde Fjord near Skuldelev in Denmark.** © *Ted Spiegel/CORBIS*

RIGHT: **Parts of the Oseberg ship are highly decorated.** *Hulton Getty Picture Collection*

LEFT: **Fashioned from gilded bronze, elaborate weather vanes like this 11th century example were mounted in Viking longships to provide information on the bearing and strength of the wind.** ©*Archivo Iconografico, S.A./CORBIS*

While Norse longships were among the most distinctive vessels of their day, they also represented a dead-end in warship development. Improvements in sailing rigs and the inherent vulnerability of oared vessels in battle, led to the gradual abandonment of the longship during the 10th to 12th centuries. In the Bayeaux Tapestry, William the Conqueror's invasion fleet partially consisted of longships, with oar-holes along their hull. Like the cargo vessels shown transporting soldiers, horses and military equipment, these longships carried no oarsmen, but were powered by wind and sail, and as with the "lyfting" on Norse longships, these Norman vessels had raised stern platforms, a feature which would eventually develop into the sterncastle. Over the next two centuries, longships disappeared, although oared warships continued to be used in the Mediterranean by the Byzantines and Moors.

The best evidence for contemporary ship design comes from surviving coins and seals. In the period from the 10th to the 12th centuries, the "knorr" design developed, as ships became larger, hulls became more rounded, and decks were planked over, creating cargo holds. These were the craft used by the Crusaders as they sailed to the Holy Land, and served as troop transports and warships as well as cargo carriers. Two seals from the English town of Hastings show small clinker-built wooden vessels with temporary "castle" structures at the stern, and sometimes both bow and stern. A platform or "top" was fitted to the masthead, to serve as

a lookout post or as a fighting platform. A 13th century seal produced in the crusading port of Acre shows a similar vessel, but with a more permanent bow and stern castle and fighting top. Crossbowmen occupy the waist and sterncastle, while seamen throwing rocks are shown in the fighting top. At some time during the late 12th century the rudder was moved from the starboard side of these vessels to the stern. This development coincided with the introduction of the bowsprit, and the combination made ships far more maneuvrable under sail. In 1962 the remains of a vessel dating from c1329 was discovered off the German port of Bremen. This vessel type was known as a "cog," and formed the standard form of craft found in Northern European waters during the medieval period. These craft have been associated with the bustling ports of northern Germany, and are depicted on seals of the ports run by the Hanseatic League. Similar vessels were used throughout Europe, as evidenced by port seals and manuscript illustrations. Their characteristics were a barrel-like hull, with a permanent stern structure, a decked-over cargo hold and a single mast and square sail. It had a very high freeboard, a stern rudder, and sharply inclined stem and stern posts. Although primarily a cargo vessel, cogs could be fitted with fighting platforms at the bow and stern, and turned into a warship. During the 14th century the stern structure became larger, while the forecastle became smaller, and the sterncastles merged into the hull of the ship. A mid-14th century

LEFT AND RIGHT: **Two fanciful images of the longship — each with its dragon head and sail and oar combination. That at left shows Olaf Anlaff's fleet entering the Humber. In reality, dragon prows were rare, and were probably only used on the largest and most prestigious of the Viking longships.** *Hulton Getty Picture Collection*

33

ABOVE: **Although fanciful, this 19th century representation of Viking raiders shows them rowing a craft similar to those used by the earliest Saxon raiders during the 5th century AD.** *Hulton Getty Picture Collection*

LEFT: **An overturned longship on display at L'Anse aux Meadows National Historic Site, where the Vikings first settled.** *©Greg Probst/CORBIS*

RIGHT: **Although extremely inaccurate, this representation of a Viking fleet evokes an impression of the fear which the coastal communities must have felt when these ships appeared off their shores. From an oil painting, "Viking ships in a rough sea" by Edward Moran.** *©Bettmann/CORBIS*

BELOW: **These Bronze Age rock carvings of pre-Norse vessels from Tanum in Sweden are typical of hundreds of similar representations which survive throughout Scandinavia.** *©Carmen Redondo/CORBIS*

LEFT: **This 7th century AD limestone plinth from the Swedish island of Gotland clearly depicts the paneled square sail used by the Norse raiders.** *©Archivo Iconografico, S.A./CORBIS*

RIGHT: **The American Viking replica ship, the *Snorri*, sails the rugged Newfoundland coastline near the fishing village of L'Anse aux Meadows, July 27, 2000.** *©Reuters NewMedia Inc./CORBIS*

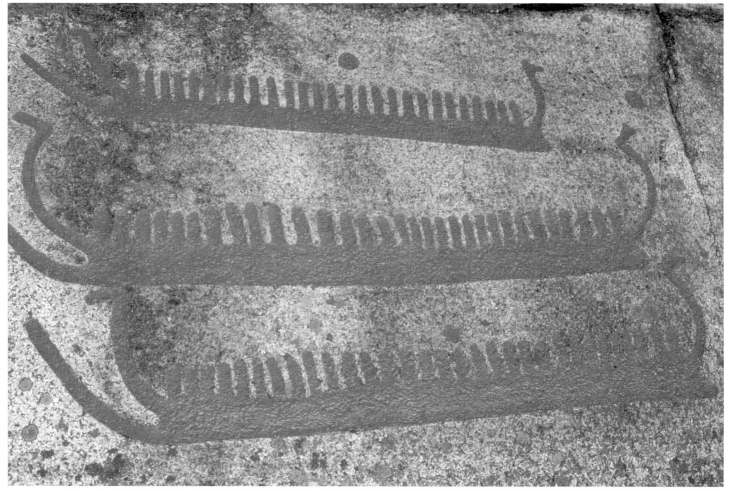

Battle of Sluys

The 100 Years' War between England and France arose out of the disputed inheritance to the French crown, both Edward III of England and Philip VI of France claiming legitimacy. At the start of the war Philip VI planned to invade England, mobilizing a fleet. Approximately 200 ships were gathered at Sluys in Flanders under the command of Sir Hugh Kiriet, manned by French and Castilian knights and including a squadron of Genoese galleys led by Admiral Babbaveria, and some Flemish privateers. Edward gathered a fleet in England and in June 1340 sailed from Ipswich in his flagship *Thomas* with approximately 250 ships. He anchored off Sluys on the 23rd, making contact with the Flemish on land, then soon after dawn on June 24 the battle started. The French ships were tightly crammed into a channel, arranged in three lines chained together to form a defensive barrier. This surrendering of the initiative caused Babbaveria to withdraw his galleys in protest. The English ships attacked in three divisions, surrounding the French ships, which were unable to maneuver. Edward had crammed two out of every three ships with longbowmen, the third being full of men at arms, and from the towering castles on the ships the archers set up a murderous hail of arrows on to the French decks. The melee that followed lasted much of the day, but the French were routed, losing up to 190 ships and an estimated 25,000 men (those forced ashore being butchered by the Flemings), against 4,500 English losses. The Battle of Sluys removed any further French threat of invasion in the war and allowed Edward to land expeditionary forces in France at will.

illustration showing a cog filled with soldiers has archers sited on the large sterncastle, and swordsmen in the waist and forecastle. These fore and stern castles were often shown to be crenelated like contemporary castles, emphasizing the fortress-like qualities of these structures. This coincided with the addition of extra masts to Northern European ships, following the example of Mediterranean ships which carried mizzen masts fitted with lateen sails. From the early 15th century, small foremasts were fitted to forecastle structures.

The largest sea battle fought in Northern European waters took place at Sluys in 1340. A contemporary depiction of the engagement shows both sides using cogs, where archers occupied the two castles and the fighting tops, while swordsmen and spearmen formed boarding parties in the waist of the ships. War at sea was simply an extension of combat on land, with men-at-arms supported by archers. The mid-14th century also saw the arrival of artillery on the medieval battlefield, and it is virtually certain that handguns were employed on board ship soon afterwards. In 1380 a manuscript records that a warship from Pisa carried gunners, and handgunners are shown in a depiction of a sea battle between the Venetians and supporters of the Holy Roman Emperor. Firearms of sorts were employed in the Mediterranean from the seventh century AD, when the Byzantines used "Greek fire" during a battle with the Persians (628AD). This was an incendiary weapon, based on naptha was developed by the Romans, to be used during sieges. The Byzantines developed a cannon-like naptha projector, and continued to use the device until the 15th century. There is no recorded instance of Greek fire being used in Northern European waters.

Another exclusively Mediterranean feature was the re-emergence of the war galley. The Byzantines had used small biremes (called "dromons") from the 5th until the 14th century, and a 14th century painting from Sienna shows a sea battle between galley fleets. Unlike the galleys of the Ancient World, tactics seem to have been limited to boarding, and were therefore similar to those used between fleets of sailing vessels of the same period.

Galleys continued to be used by the Italian city states during the 14th and 15th centuries, and artillery was employed on these galleys from 1380. Around 1500 the quantity of oars were reduced and the number of oarsmen increased, from two to four or five. Artillery was mounted in a platform over the stem, with the largest guns closest to the centerline. While smaller galley variants existed, naval power in the Mediterranean during the 16th century centred around fleets of these large war galleys.

Although a handful of galleys were built in northern Europe during this period, the experiment was unsuccessful, and galley warfare remained a Mediterranean phenomenon.

The great religious conflict between Christians and Moslems in the Mediterranean basin reached a climax during the mid-16th century, and resulted in the great naval engagement at Lepanto (1571). A coalition of Christian states (principally Venice, Spain, Naples and the Papacy) defeated an Ottoman Turkish fleet in a dramatic clash between two galley fleets. Tactics revolved around the destruction of ships through firepower and ramming, although both sides also resorted to hand-to-hand combat. The Christian superiority in artillery proved decisive, and from that point on, gunnery dominated naval warfare.

The 15th century saw the first evidence of the mounting of artillery into sailing ships, first in the form of light swivel guns, and later by the employment of light "bombards." Henry V of England's warship *Grace Dieu* built before 1420 was fitted with both "serpentynes" (swivel guns) and "curows" (light bombards), while Hanseatic vessels carried similar weapons to deter pirates. The design of late

Battle of Lepanto

The Battle of Lepanto in 1571 was the largest naval engagement since Actium in 31BC and was the last great battle between galleys. The Ottoman Turks had embarked on a campaign to take over Venetian possessions in the eastern Mediterranean and invaded Cyprus in 1570. The next year Venice formed an alliance with Philip II of Spain and Pope Pius V and a combined fleet of the Holy League, under the command of Don John of Austria, assembled in Sicily. Following the invasion of Cyprus, the Turkish fleet, commanded by Ali Pasa, entered the Adriatic and lay off Greece in the mouth of the Gulf of Patras, near Lepanto. On October 7, 1571, the Holy League fleet encountered the Ottoman ships and advanced in four squadrons, Ali Pasa's fleet in turn attacking in a crescent formation. The fleets were evenly matched with figures given for the Holy League fleet listing 200 galleys and 80,000 men on board (of which 50,000 were rowers and 30,000 infantry, many of whom were Spanish). The fighting was often at close quarters but gunfire was also used, from both ship-mounted guns and arquebuses carried by the infantry. The Venetians had six galleasses, which were particularly effective. Larger than the galleon, they had to be towed into battle, but once in position their size meant that they provided a powerful, stable gun platform. After four hours of fighting, the Holy League captured the Ottoman flagship, killed Ali Pasa, and the defeated Ottoman ships retreated. The aura of Ottoman naval invincibility had been broken, Lepanto being its first defeat. The Ottoman fleet had been destroyed and between 15,000 and 25,000 Ottoman sailors lost their lives. The Holy League lost 7,000 men but liberated 10,000-12,000 Christian galley slaves.

The Battle of Lepanto was a decisive victory for the Christian galley fleets of the Mediterranean. This oil painting in the Civic Museum of Art in Venice commemorated the part played by the Italian city state in the battle.
©*Archivo Iconografico, S.A./CORBIS*

Don John of Austria

Don John of Austria (1547-78) was the illegitimate son of the Holy Roman Emperor Charles V. When Philip II of Spain succeeded to his father Charles' throne, he established his half-brother Don John as a military commander. His naval training started in 1568 when he fought Moorish pirates in the Mediterranean, before returning to Spain in 1569 to put down the Morisco uprising in Granada. In 1571 Don John achieved his greatest victory, crushing the Ottoman Turks' fleet at the Battle of Lepanto. The battle was the last great battle under oar. The Turkish fleet had up to then never suffered defeat and was threatening further conquests in the eastern Mediterranean. Appointed by Philip II to lead the naval forces of Spain, Venice and the pope, Don John was able to use his influence to unite the various fleets and admirals of the Holy League fleet into a powerful naval force. After his victory at Lepanto, Don John continued to press the Turks, taking Tunis in 1573, but was then withdrawn by his brother. In 1576 he was made governor-general of the Netherlands, where he had plans to invade England, but reverted to warfare in the face of the rebellion in the Netherlands against Spanish rule, dying in 1578 at Bouges, near Namur, which he had captured the previous year.

ABOVE: **Portrait of Don John of Austria from a woodcut by E. Van Leest.** ©*Bettmann/CORBIS*

BELOW: **Don John's tomb is in the monastery of El Escorial, Spain.** ©*Adam Woolfitt/CORBIS*

LEFT: **The Henry Grâce à Dieu, a 17th century representation of the 16th century warship.**
TRH Pictures

medieval ships was changing, partly due to an amalgam of the shipbuilding traditions of northern and southern Europe. Three-masted square-rigged ships were now common throughout Europe, but the clinker-built hull remained an exclusively northern European feature. Both regions produced vessels known as "carracks" (or naos) which were improvements over the older cog design. They carried three masts, with pronounced forecastle and sterncastle structures, rounded hulls and squared sterns. This design also permitted the carrying of large pieces of ordnance. The Flemish artist "WA" painted a "kraek" (carrack) in 1470, fitted with anti-boarding screens in the castles and swivel guns in the fighting tops. By 1500, a depiction of a Venetian carrack was shown with holes cut in the side for larger guns, and an account of an Anglo-French sea battle off Brest in 1515 mentioned the use of heavy bombards. Clearly, by 1500 large guns were being introduced onto ships, which altered the way naval warfare was conducted. Until that point, naval battles consisted of exchanging archery volleys, then closing to board the enemy. For the first time, warships had the ability to avoid contact and fight battles without boarding. For much of the 16th century, naval doctrine would struggle to catch up the technical improvements offered by the introduction of artillery into warships.

The introduction of gunports around 1510 led to a change in the way carracks were constructed. Clinker-built hulls were weakened by cutting holes in the hull, so warships designed from the keel up to carry ordnance were built using carvel construction, with the planks laid edge to edge.

The Tudor warship *Mary Rose*, built in 1515, was a powerful royal warship, and was a true carrack. She was refitted in 1536 to support the carrying of even heavier guns, and this over-arming was a contributing factor in her accidental loss in 1545. The *Mary Rose* was discovered and excavated, and her hull is now on display in a special museum in Portsmouth, on England's south coast. Her armament was a mixture of modern bronze guns mounted on four-wheeled carriages to older wrought-iron pieces, on two-wheeled sleds. Although equipped with a powerful broadside armament, she also carried light swivel guns, and a full complement of archers and other soldiers. The tactics of the time were still based on fighting a boarding action, where the great guns were fired to disrupt the enemy prior to grappling and boarding, under a covering fire from the archers. When the Portuguese explorer Vasco da Gama fought off an attack by Indian craft in 1500, he used artillery fire to keep the enemy at a distance. Like any technical innovation, it took time for military and naval commanders to understand how use the new technology to their advantage.

Golden Age of Sail
BROADSIDES AND GALLEONS

By 1550, most of the technical problems created by the introduction of artillery into warships had been overcome. Although the armament of 16th century warships was far from being homogenous, these vessels were similar in basic layout to those found in the navies of Britain, France and Spain some 250 years later. They carried most of their ordnance in broadside batteries, capable of delivering a heavy blow to enemy vessels. Unfortunately, it took a century for naval tacticians to discover the best way to use the tools they had been given.

From the time the English warship *Mary Rose* sank in 1545 until the end of the 17th century, warship design was influenced by two considerations. The first was the growing interest in the creation of prestigious ships and powerful navies. The expansion of European interests overseas led to the need for fleets capable of fighting the nation's enemies on the far side of the world if required. The second was the realization that artillery was the arbiter of victory in naval

BELOW: **The English fleet harries the Spanish Armada as it passes Plymouth. In the center is a likeness of Charles Howard, Lord Efffingham, who commanded the English forces.** *Bison Picture Library*

The Armada

In the late 1580s Philip II of Spain began to build up an armada to invade England in an attempt to resolve the long-running war with Queen Elizabeth I. On May 30, 1588, the Spanish Armada of 150 ships left Lisbon under the command of the Duke of Medina-Sidonia. Progress was slow against unfavorable winds and after being forced into Corunna to resupply, the armada reached the Channel on July 28. The British fleet, under the command of Lord Howard of Effingham with Francis Drake as his vice-admiral, ably supported by Frobisher and Hawkins, first spotted the armada the next day, setting sail from its base in Plymouth to track the Armada up the Channel on the 30th. Although the Spanish had the numerical advantage in warships, plus a huge number of armed merchantmen, and their galleons were larger, favoring close-combat, the British ships were nimbler, with long guns and more effective gunners, enabling them to fight a stand-off artillery duel. The first clash came on July 31 when the British attacked the armada off Plymouth, the Spanish ships arranged in crescent-moon formation suffering some damage to four ships, two of which were captured. The strength of the armada meant that the British determined on harrying it, although during the next engagement, on August 2 off Portland, the English ships engaged more closely to maximize the effectiveness of their guns, although the encounter again produced only light casualties. For the next four days the English harried the Spanish as the wind blew them up the Channel until both fleets anchored off Calais on August 6. The fiercest battle in the Armada's course took place north of Calais, off Gravelines on August 8, and the Spanish suffered 1,400 casualties to the 300 lost by the English, being pushed further north. At this stage Medina-Sidonia decided that he would be unable to land his invasion forces and decided to run for Spain around Scotland. The armada was almost completely destroyed by storms off southwest Ireland, Medina-Sidonia reaching northern Spain on September 21 with only 65 ships eventually returning.

combat. The *Mary Rose* carried a motley collection of guns which varied in size, range and effectiveness. By the end of the 16th century, all major warships carried bronze or cast-iron guns, arranged into homogenous batteries.

The *Mary Rose* was a carrack, and the only difference between her and a merchant vessel was her armament and size of crew. During the Spanish Armada of 1588, most of the Spanish fleet consisted of merchantmen converted into warships by adding guns to them. Similarly, although the nucleus of the English navy consisted of specially designed warships, the bulk of the fleet were armed merchantmen, hired for the occasion. The exceptions to this were the truly revolutionary warships which formed the core of both fleets in 1588. These vessels were known as "galleons."

The galleon was a seagoing, fully-rigged ship characterized by a high ratio of length to breadth, fine lines and a pronounced forecastle and sterncastle. They were less clumsy than carracks, having less superstructure, and they were usually well-armed. They were almost exclusively a Spanish phenomenon, although the English developed a variant known as a "race-built" galleon in time for the

RIGHT: **"English ships and the Spanish Armada, August 1588." An oil painting by an unknown artist of the English school, late 16th century. The painting is in the collection of the National Maritime Museum, Greenwich, London. In the foreground is one of the four-oared galleasses used by the Spanish.** ©*Bettmann/CORBIS*

Sir Francis Drake

Sir Francis Drake (c1540-96) was the greatest English seaman of the golden age of Elizabethan seafaring. In his first major expedition in 1567 he commanded the *Judith* as part of his kinsman John Hawkins' largely unsuccessful attempt to wrest territory from the Spanish in the West Indies. In 1577 he set off on an epic voyage to the Pacific, starting with five ships but after storms and fire devastated his fleet rounding South America, through the Strait of Magellan, he continued alone in the *Golden Hind*, later rounding the Cape of Good Hope in Africa and returning to England in 1580. In recognition of his exploits, he was knighted on board the *Golden Hind* by Queen Elizabeth I. He continued to lead the conflict against Spain, taking 25 ships to the Spanish Indies in 1585 to return with native produce and a failed colony of English settlers from Virginia. Two years later, in 1587, he raided the Spanish fleet at Cadiz, setting fire to the ships at anchor and when the Spanish Armada attempted to invade England in 1588 he was appointed vice-admiral of the English fleet as it harried the Spaniards for a week along the Channel. His final trip was again to the Spanish West Indies, where he died on board ship near Puerto Bello, Panama, of dysentery in 1596.

Armada campaign, and the French and Italian states also built their own variants. The first Spanish galleons were designed to escort the annual treasure "flotas," ensuring that the Spanish crown received a steady flow of silver from the New World. These galleons were solid ships; braced and reinforced to weather repeated transatlantic crossings, and fitted with four masts. Their role as a warship was secondary to their primary function as an armed carrier of specie. The rest of the fleet consisted of armed merchant carracks (naos) and their lighter counterpart, the "caravel."

Sir Francis Drake is remembered as one of England's finest naval commanders, even though he rarely served in the Queen's navy. Instead, he conducted nationally sanctioned raids against the Spanish on the New World. The real arbiter of victory was John Hawkins, a "sea dog" who became the leading naval administrator in the decade leading up to the Armada campaign. Hawkins refitted the older warships of the Tudor navy by cutting down their superstructure, fitting more guns and improving handling qualities. He also worked with naval architects such as Matthew Baker to produce England's own version of the galleon. These English "race-built" galleons were lower, faster and more maneuverable than their Spanish counterparts.

While the majority of the Spanish ships used bronze muzzle-loading guns, some converted merchantmen were still armed with obsolete wrought-iron breech-loading pieces. Even worse, the Spanish sea carriages were fitted with two large wheels, resembling the field carriages found on land. By contrast, English guns were mounted on four-wheeled carriages similar to those used by all navies into the 19th century. The English system was quicker to operate. During the campaign the Spanish tried to fight in the old manner, firing a broadside before attempting to board their opponent. The English avoided contact, relying on gunnery to batter their opponent. Although few Spanish ships were lost through English gunnery, the superiority of the English system was demonstrated. From that point on, gunnery would become the accepted mode of naval combat.

At the start of the 17th century, Spain was still the dominant maritime power in the world. Her losses of 1588 had

LEFT: **Sir Francis Drake (c.1540-1596), in a depiction by an 18th century engraver.** *©Michael Nicholson/CORBIS*

ABOVE RIGHT: **Drake leading his men in an attack on Puerto Rico in late 1595. The "seadog" launched two attacks on the Spanish port that year, and both were repulsed.** *©Bettmann/CORBIS*

RIGHT: **"Drake attacking a treasure ship," a 19th century engraving purporting to represent Drake's capture of the Spanish galleon *Nuestra Señora de Rosario* in 1588.** *©Bettmann/CORBIS*

LEFT: **The *Sovereign of the Seas*, Phineas Pett's most impressive prestige warship, built for Charles I.**
TRH Pictures

been replaced by a new breed of galleons, closely modeled on their English "race-built" counterparts. The treasure galleon *Nuestra Señora de Atocha* lost in 1622 was typical of this new breed. She displaced 500 tons, carried 22 modern guns and was crewed by a mixture of sailors and veteran soldiers. She was a modest, practical galleon, designed to perform the specific function of carrying treasure and escorting merchantmen. By contrast, while the Spanish concentrated on the practicalities of naval design, other European developed warships more for their imposing appearance than for any practical function they might serve.

In 1610 the English shipwright Phineas Pett built the *Prince Royal*, the first of a series of large, prestigious warships commissioned by European rulers during the first half of the 17th century. The production of immense warships was an empirical process, as factors such as stability and optimal sailing plans were still not fully understood. Pett's flagship was designed as the largest and most prestigious warship in the world, and her armament of 56 guns seemed less important than her splendid decoration. She also boasted three gundecks, marking a new departure in the development of ships as floating gun batteries. Her launch spurred other European rulers to commission their own prestigious flagships. The French 60-gun *St. Louis* launched a decade later was only a two-decker, but she was equally ostentatious, combining gunpower with prestigious design. King Gustavus Vasa of Sweden was not to be outdone, as Sweden considered herself the greatest naval power in the Baltic region. He commissioned Dutch shipwrights to build a warship with two gundecks, but the king constantly interfered with its design, creating a ship which was top-heavy and insufficiently ballasted to support her sail plan.

The 80-ton warship *Vasa* (*Wasa*) was fitted out in Stockholm harbor in 1628, and the King came to see her set sail on her maiden voyage. Inside the harbor the wind caught her sails, and when she heeled over, water flooded in through her open gunports, which were set too low in the hull. The *Vasa* keeled over and sank, taking most of her crew with her.

The wreck was rediscovered in 1961 and raised from the seabed. After extensive conservation, her virtually intact hull is on display in a specially constructed museum, a monument to the golden age of sail, and to the ego and folly of the Swedish monarch. Much of the decoration of this three-decked 64-gun warship survived, and it is evident that this embellishment only added to the stability problems.

The epitome of these prestigious warships was the *Sovereign of the Seas*, famous for being a leading contributor to the outbreak of the English Civil War in 1642, due to opposition to the "Ship Tax" imposed to pay for her construction. In 1634 King Charles I instructed Phineas Pett design the largest warship in the world. She was launched three years later, and was the most impressive of all the prestige warships, having a keel of 127 feet, a beam of 46 feet and a displacement of over 1,500 tons. She also carried 100 guns, making her the most powerful warship afloat.

The king had little chance to enjoy his flagship, as when Civil War erupted in 1642, the renamed *Royal Sovereign* was claimed by Parliament, and spent the conflict operating against the King. When most of her ostentatious gilding, carving and other decoration was removed, she proved a solid, reliable warship, and continued in service until 1696, when she was destroyed by an accidental fire on board. During this time her superstructure was cut down to conform to the latest trends in warship design, and she was refitted to take a smaller but heavier suite of ordnance.

Throughout the 17th century, the tendency was to reduce the height of warships, and to almost completely do away with the forecastle. A series of naval wars between the English and the Dutch during the mid- to late-17th century demonstrated a growing commitment to the production of functional warships rather than the creation of prestigious ones. The *Sovereign of the Seas* acted as a prototype for a series of three-decked warships produced by England and France during this period, becoming the "first-rate" warships of the 18th century. The majority of the English and French fleets consisted of two-deckers, as they provided the most cost-effective size of vessel. As for the Dutch, the shallow coastal waters of their coastline precluded the use of these larger warships, and most Dutch ships were two-deckers or less, with a lighter armament and a shallower draught than their English counterparts. During this period the Dutch were seen as the foremost experts in ship design, and their shipwrights were in constant demand by other European powers. The mid-17th century also saw the creation of a new type of warship. The "frigate" was a small, fast vessel with a single gundeck. Faster and more maneuverable than the larger "ships of the line," these vessels became a vital part of the national navies of the era.

The period from 1650 until 1815 saw a series of seemingly continuous wars in Europe, and most of these involved one or more of the leading maritime powers; France, Spain, Holland and England (Britain after 1707). All of these nations maintained colonies or trading links overseas, and in time of war the safeguard of maritime commerce was a necessity. These large standing navies were a new phenomenon. Before the mid-17th century, most navies consisted of a nucleus of royal warships, and armed merchantmen were hired to augment this force in time of war. By 1650, navies were built, owned and maintained by the state. Powerful navies were vital in safeguarding national interests in wartime, and during peace they acted as a "fleet-in-being," serving as a deterrent to rival powers.

Equally important was the role played by these warships. At the start of the Dutch Wars, fleets sailed into action in no particular formation, and once battle commenced, it became a free-for-all. During the First Dutch War (1654-55), the Generals-at-Sea of England's Commonwealth developed a tactic that better suited the ships they commanded. Contemporary warships carried almost all of their armament in broadside batteries, protected by thick wooden hulls. The weak points were the bow and the stern, where "raking fire" could smash through the entire length of a gundeck. To avoid this, Commonwealth

RIGHT: **Admiral Michiel de Ruyter.** *TRH Pictures*

De Ruyter

Seventeenth century Holland was a leading European power, its influence stretching around the globe through its large navy and extensive trade links. Admiral Michiel de Ruyter (1607-76), one of the greatest Dutch seamen of his age, led the navy in its numerous wars with competing nations. In the first Anglo-Dutch War (1652-54) the Dutch suffered mounting heavy losses and afterward de Ruyter was influential in pressing for a massive rebuilding program of larger ships to combat the English. Although the Dutch continued to build up their navy, when the second Anglo-Dutch War was declared (1664-67), it was still outgunned by the Royal Navy. Although both sides suffered losses in a sequence of large sea battles, the Dutch blockade was effective in blunting England's naval effort, and peace was signed after de Ruyter led a daring raid up the Medway in June 1667, burning Royal Navy vessels and installations at Chatham and towing away the English flagship, *Royal Charles*. War broke out again in 1672, when France and England attacked Holland. Although outmatched, de Ruyter as Commander-in-Chief of the Dutch navy, defeated the English fleet in the Battle of Sole Bay on June 6, 1672, preventing it assisting in the invasion of Holland. The following year de Ruyter fought a superb defensive campaign, using the greater speed and mobility of his forces to defeat a larger Anglo-French force off Zeeland in two battles in June and shattering a superior Anglo-French invasion force (5,386 guns against 3,667 guns) off Texel. Again England was forced to sue for peace in 1674. Now a national hero, de Ruyter died of wounds sustained in action against the French in the Mediterranean in 1676.

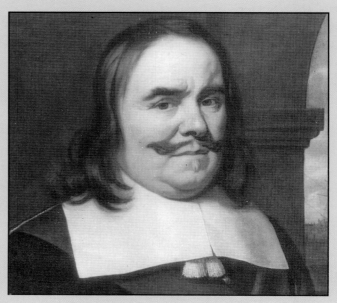

commanders such as Robert Blake and Richard Deane developed the "line-of-battle." The larger warships followed each other into battle, taking signals and course changes from the leading ship, which was usually the flagship. This reduced the risk of raking fire, and presented a massed series of broadside batteries to the enemy. Smaller vessels such as frigates were gradually kept out of the line-of-battle, and relegated to scouting, escort and commerce-raiding missions.

By the late 17th century, the large vessels which formed these lines-of-battle became known as ships of the line. Sailing warships were rarely sunk in action, but were battered, dismasted and forced to surrender. The line-of-battle reduced the risk of enemy vessels combining forces against solitary friendly warships, and allowed fleets to disengage when the admiral in command deemed it prudent. By the early 18th century, a rigid adherence to the maintenance of this line was considered of paramount importance, leading to a stalemate in naval tactics. The line-of-battle discouraged risk, and battles therefore became inconclusive. Most of the spectacular victories during the golden age of sail took place when one side deliberately or accidentally broke the rules.

The Dutch Wars also served as an impetus for the classification of warships. From the 1660s, warships were grouped into classes, graded according to the number if guns they carried. A "First Rate" had over 90 guns, and were the direct descendants of the prestige warships such as the *Sovereign of the Seas*. A "Second Rate" carried between 80 and 90 guns, while a "Third Rate" carried more than 50.

Battle of Quiberon Bay

During the Seven Years War (1756-63), the two great colonial powers, England and France, were engaged in a struggle for dominance in North America and Europe. In 1759 the French were building up an invasion force at Morbihan in Brittany, while the Royal Navy under Admiral Hawke blockaded the French fleet at Brest. In November, the French commander, Admiral de Conflans, took advantage of gales to finally leave port, but on November 20 was sighted by Hawke's fleet off Belle-Ile near Morbihan.

In stormy conditions Hawke gave chase as the French ran for shelter downwind into the bay. Conflans intended to form a defensive line if the British followed into the unfamiliar, dangerous waters but Hawke, ordering his ships to raise full sail, caught the French rear as it entered the bay. In the high seas, with little room between rocks and shoals, the fighting became a melee, but superior British seamanship began to tell. Conflans attempted to take the van of his fleet out of the bay again but as night fell was forced to anchor and the fighting died down. The next morning the full extent of the destruction of the French invasion fleet was revealed. The British had lost two ships and suffered approximately 300 casualties; the French had lost seven ships and 2,500 men.

These three classes constituted all the ships which were considered large enough to sail in line-of-battle, and henceforward were given the collective name of "ships of the line." A "Fourth Rate" was a smaller (non line-of-battle) ship with over 38 guns, while below it a "Fifth Rate" carried 18-38 guns, and a "Sixth Rate" from 6-18. Smaller vessels were "Unrated." Of the smaller rates, most frigates were Fifth Rates, and smaller vessels included brigs, sloops and cutters. This classification remained in use until after the end of the Napoleonic Wars in 1815, with one exception. During the 18th century, as warships increased in size and power, smaller Third Rates were deemed too small to remain in the line-of-battle. By the 1750s, 50-gun Third Rates were rarely employed, and by 1795, most Third Rates carried 70 guns or more, the most common being the 74-gun ship of the line. During the same period frigates increased in size, and most became Fourth Rates. Second Rates became rare after a spurt of popularity in the late 17th century, and most ships of the line were either First or Third Rates.

At the start of the 18th century, the basic classification, appearance and role of sailing warships had been established, and would continue in use until well into the following century. While certain changes in sailing configuration and design took place, most modifications resulted from the constant desire to carry heavier armament, and to create stable gun platforms from which the ordnance could be operated. During the late 17th century, the design of English ships was considered inferior to those built in Spain, France or Holland. Although English shipwrights copied the designs of captured ships, the same was true of English warship design of the 18th century. Within a decade of 1700, all major warships went through certain design changes instituted by the French and Dutch shipwrights. The "spritsail topmast," which extended vertically from the end of bowsprit, was removed, and replaced with an extended bowsprit, capable of carrying an extra jib. During the 18th century, the lateen sail which was carried on the mizzen mast was gradually replaced with a gaff-rigged sail, which was more responsive and easier to handle. From about 1710 on, warships of all rates were built with smaller forecastles, and a less pronounced series of steps in the sterncastle structure. The longest of these was the quarter-deck, which in most cases replaced any smaller poop deck arrangement further aft. In France and Holland, warships were built with a wider beam than found in English ships, making them more stable as gun platforms, particularly in rough conditions.

Outside the British Isles the study of warship design was considered an important science, leading to the production of detailed plans, shipbuilding treatises and consequently, more stable ships, capable of operating anywhere in the world. Although Admiralty ship models were used to introduce some conformity from 1660 onward, ship design in England (or Britain from 1707) remained an empirical process, and good designs were found as a result of trial and error. More often than not, these were found by copying the designs of captured foreign warships. This had the effect of reducing the effect of national characteristics in warship design as the 18th century progressed. In 1768 the portfolio

LEFT: "The Battle of Quiberon Bay, 21st November 1759: the day after." Oil painting by Richard Wright (1735-1775). The painting is in the collection of the National Maritime Museum, Greenwich, London. *via TRH Pictures*

RIGHT: Commodore Perry's victory at the battle of Lake Erie, September 10, 1813, from an American engraving. *Chrysalis Images*

Battle of Chesapeake Bay

The American War of Independence (1775-83) drew French and Americans together against a common enemy — Britain. In 1781 a British army under Lord Cornwallis was faced at Yorktown, Virginia, near Chesapeake Bay, by a colonial force commanded by Lafayette. Naval supply was vital to both sides. A French naval squadron led by de Grasse eluded the British in the Caribbean and sailed north to reach the Chesapeake at the end of August. On September 5 a combined British squadron under the command of Rear Admiral Thomas Graves, with Rear Admiral Samuel Hood's squadron from the West Indies, arrived at Chesapeake Bay. Its strength of 19 ships of the line and one 50-gun ship compared unfavorably with de Grasse's 24 ships of the line and two frigates. De Grasse set sail for the open sea as soon as possible, ordering his ships to rapidly form a battle line at 12.30pm. A series of confusing signals from Graves hampered the British attempt to form a parallel battle line moving in the opposite direction to the French, and the van of the British ships bore obliquely down on the French, with firing beginning on the leading ships soon after 4pm. The head of the British line bore the brunt of the concerted French fire as Graves, leading the center, was unable to engage. As night fell, c6:30pm, the French bore away and although both sides had suffered heavy casualties, the British also had several ships incapacitated. For the next few days both fleets attempted to repair the damage without attempting to engage each other and when de Grasse re-entered the Chesapeake on September 11, he joined another French squadron led by de Barras, giving the French the advantage of 36 ships to 18 of the line. Graves sailed to New York for reinforcements but on October 19, before he could return, Cornwallis was forced to surrender his forces to George Washington and the final defeat of the British in America was in sight.

of warship and merchant ship designs published by the Anglo-Swedish shipwright Frederik Henrik Chapman (*Architectura Navalis Mercatoria*) helped consolidate the lessons learned in improving ship stability, speed and strength. As Europe entered the French Revolutionary and Napoleonic Wars (1795-1815), the main battlefleets of all the major protagonists consisted of warships which were relatively similar, irrespective of who built them or where. Certain exceptions were more commonly due to the use of poor materials or shoddy construction than to any inherent design flaws. Once again, British shipyards seemed to lag behind their continental rivals in the reliability of the warships they produced.

Frigates grew in importance during the 18th century, and although guns were still mounted on a single deck, the size and weight of the armament increased. By 1760, most frigates carried between 30 and 36 guns (mainly 12-pounders). By 1815, most frigates carried over 40 guns, making them powerful commerce raiders and escorts. Scouting and communications were left to smaller vessels such as 18-gun sloops or brigs. During the War of 1812 (1812-15) between Britain and the United States, the American fleet contained three "super-frigates", armed with 30 24-pounders and 20 12-pounders. Ship for ship, these vessels proved superior to any British frigate they encountered. In addition to these "Rated" warships, fleets

RIGHT: **Continental Navy schooner, the eight-gun** *Wasp* **(1775-77).** *TRH Pictures/US Navy*

FAR RIGHT: **USS** *Alfred* **(1775-78) flagship of the Continental Navy.** *TRH Pictures/US Navy*

ABOVE LEFT: **The *Bonhomme Richard* (formerly the East-Indiaman *Duc de Duras*), of 1779 was a 40-gun frigate.** *Chrysalis Images*

BELOW LEFT: Bonhomme Richard **will always be remembered for its battle against the British *Serapis*, John Paul Jones' famous victory of September 21, 1779. This is from the painting by James Hamilton.** *Chrysalis Images*

ABOVE: **The duel between the frigates USS *Chesapeake* and HMS *Shannon*, June 1, 1813. After a brief but vicious fight, the British warship was victorious.** *Chrysalis Images*

RIGHT: **The USS *Constitution*, a 44-gun American frigate which was more powerful than any frigate the British possessed in 1812. Oil painting by Marshall Johnson.** *Chrysalis Images*

Victory

HMS *Victory* is the only surviving example of a Royal Navy First Rate ship of the line. The enormous cost of building and maintaining these ships, with a crew of up to 850, meant that a total of only 34 100+ gun three-decker British First Rates were built, the first being King Charles I's *Sovereign of the Seas* in 1637; the last, *Trafalgar*, was launched in 1841. The keel of HMS *Victory* was laid down in 1759, during the Seven Years' War, following the design of Sir Thomas Slade, Surveyor of the Navy, but she was not floated until 1765. Her masts, sails and rigging were then completed and sea trials were carried out in 1769. However, she was not commissioned until 1778, becoming the flagship of Admiral Keppel for the Channel Fleet. Her first engagement was at the battle of Ushant that year against a French fleet, and subsequently she had to return to Plymouth for minor repairs. She followed the usual practice of service, refits (copper sheathing being fitted to her hull) and repairs, being transferred to the Mediterranean Fleet in 1793, where she was Admiral Jervis' flagship at the Battle of Cape St. Vincent in 1797. Her most famous moment was to be Nelson's flagship at the Battle of Trafalgar in 1805, carrying his body back to England after he had died on board. Badly damaged in the battle, repaired and downrated, her active career ended in 1812, although she continued to be used as a flagship for many years. *Victory* is generally considered one of the finest First Raters as, unusually for a three-decker, she was a fine sailor and could keep up with the two-deckers making up the main body of the fleet.

Battle of Aboukir Bay

The Battle of Aboukir Bay (otherwise known as the Battle of the Nile) is regarded by many experts to be Nelson's most complete victory. Nelson had been given a squadron to chase the French fleet, under the command of Vice-Admiral Brueys, carrying Napoleon's Egyptian expeditionary force across the Mediterranean, but failed to catch it before Napoleon's army landed at Alexandria. On August 1, 1798, Nelson's fleet first sighted the French fleet at anchor unloading supplies in Aboukir Bay, east of Alexandria. Brueys had arranged the ships in a line, cabled together, stretching from the shallows at the west end of the bay. Nelson moved into action at sunset to surprise the French. The leading British ships managed to squeeze through the shallows around the head of the French line, allowing them to fire on the inner side of the French line, while Nelson took the rest of his column alongside the outside of the French ships — the bottom half of the French line, anchored and downwind, was forced to spectate. The British ships then anchored and in the ensuing devastating fire the French ships were pounded from either side. The French flagship *Orient*, in the middle of the line, was engaged by first *Bellerophon*, then *Alexander* and *Swiftsure* and at 10pm blew up with an enormous blast when her magazines exploded. Fighting continued through the night and although the French rear escaped, Nelson's victory had been complete. The opposing fleets had been roughly equal but the British had suffered approximately 800 casualties compared to estimated French losses of over 3,000. Napoleon was isolated in Egypt; British dominance of the seas had been confirmed.

also contained a myriad of small vessels, including "corvettes" for escort duties, "cutters" to relay messages and even "bomb ketches" to bombard enemy ports. Naval superiority was becoming increasingly complex, and success was determined as much by these smaller vessels as by big battle-fleets.

By the close of the 18th century, most of these fleets consisted of a handful of First Rate warships, such as HMS *Victory* (100 guns) or the Spanish *Santissima Trinidad* (120

LEFT: **HMS *Victory* is now ensconced in Portsmouth close to HMS *Warrior* and the *Mary Rose* museum, making the Historic Dockyard area a must for naval buffs.** *TRH Pictures*

ABOVE RIGHT: **Nelson's flagship HMS *Vanguard* (74-guns) following his leading ships into battle at the start of the Battle of the Aboukir Bay (also known as the Battle of the Nile), August 1, 1798.** *Hulton Getty Picture Collection*

guns), and the rest were Third Rates of 74 guns. In the Royal Navy, the "Establishment of 1780" classified the First Rate as a vessel carrying 100 guns; 32-pounders on her lower deck, 24-pounders in the middle deck, and 12-pounders on the upper deck. These vessels were served by a crew of 850 men. The Third Rate carried from 60 to 80 guns, but by 1800 the 74-gun ship of the lime became the most numerous type, as older, less homogenous warships were decommissioned. The "74" was a French design, and adapted by the British in the 1750s under the expert eye of naval architect Thomas Slade. It carried 28 32-pounders on the lower deck, and 28 18-pounders on the upper deck. The remaining guns were 9-pounders, used on the quarterdeck, or as bow or stern chasers. The introduction of carronades around 1780 altered this reliance on long guns, and the basic armament was replaced in part (or augmented) by a handful of these short-range powerful weapons. These were the vessels which took part in the Battle of the Nile (Aboukir Bay) in 1798, Copenhagen (1801) or Trafalgar (1805). Victory went to the British, not because of any technical superiority, but rather due to superior training, morale and superb leadership. Put simply, after years of training and combat, the British could fire three broadsides in the time it took for the French or Spanish to fire two. Superiority in gunnery would have little effect if both sides maintained a rigid adherence to maintaining lines-of-battle. It was the genius of British naval commanders such as Rodney, Duncan, Collingwood and Nelson that they took the gamble to break with tradition. By breaking the enemy

Nelson

The most famous naval commander in British history, Horatio Nelson (1758-1805) was a folk hero in his own lifetime. He joined the navy in 1770, in his early years commanding in the West Indies as well as Europe, where he lost the sight of his right eye in 1794 leading a naval brigade against Calvi and Bastia on Corsica. His defeat, as second-in-command to Admiral Jervis, of the Spanish fleet off Cape St Vincent in 1797 brought him fame. Later that year he was wounded in an engagement off Santa Cruz of the Canary Islands and his right arm was amputated. Arguably his most brilliant victory was when he destroyed the French fleet at the Battle of Aboukir Bay (also known as the Battle of Nile). The success of his lightning strike at sunset on the French fleet at anchor left Napoleon's force in Egypt cut-off and made Nelson an international hero. It was on his return via Naples that he first started his famous liaison with Emma, Lady Hamilton. Although both of them were married the relationship lasted until his death. In 1801 Nelson, although again second-in-command, led the successful attack on Copenhagen against the Danes, and he was finally made a commander-in-chief of the Royal Navy. Appointed vice-admiral, his victory against a combined Franco-Spanish fleet at the Battle of Trafalgar was the culmination of his career. During the battle he was shot while wearing his admiral's uniform on deck HMS *Victory* by a French marksman and died shortly afterward during the battle. His qualities of leadership, ability to communicate with his team of captains and inspire his men meant that even after his death, his orders were carried out efficiently and the subsequent victory set seal on the Royal Navy's dominance of the seas for over 100 years.

LEFT: **The surrender of the** *Redoubtable* **at the battle of Trafalgar, after a painting by William Clarkson Stanfield.**
Hulton Getty Picture Collection

INSET, LEFT: **Nelson lost his right arm during a battle with the Spanish at Santa Cruz. This engraving is after a portrait by Lemuel Abbott.**
Hulton Getty Picture Collection

Battle of Trafalgar

The Battle of Trafalgar is one of the last great sea battles of the age of sail. Napoleon's plan to invade Britain required the French fleet to decoy the Royal Navy away from home waters so that the French could hold the Channel while he crossed with his troops. In March Admiral Villeneuve took the French Mediterranean Fleet to the West Indies, with Nelson in pursuit with the British Mediterranean Fleet, but on his return he found the Brest fleet blockaded by the Royal Navy and was forced to take refuge in Cadiz. Nelson's fleet remained at Gibraltar, and on October 19 Villeneuve left Cadiz with an Allied Franco-Spanish fleet, hoping to destroy Nelson's numerically inferior force. The fleets sighted each other on October 20 off Cape Trafalgar, and at daybreak the next day the Allies formed a line of battle. Nelson, to windward, ordered his fleet to form two columns led by his flagship *Victory* and Vice-Admiral Collingwood's flagship *Royal Sovereign*, then turning to attack the Allied line. Nelson was gambling that his approaching columns would survive the Allied broadsides, which they could not return, until he broke through the enemy line and could concentrate the superior gunnery of the British to rake the bows and sterns of the Allied ships. The Allied line turned back on itself towards Cadiz, but at midday the two fleets engaged. Nelson's leading ships received heavy punishment but Collingwood took his column through the Allied line, destroying its rear. *Victory* became entangled in the line and in the fierce close-quarter battle that ensued, Nelson was killed. Again the British managed to break through the line and destroyed the Allied van. Nelson's naval genius in abandoning the conventional rigid tactics of fighting in line had reached its apotheosis. It was a crushing defeat for the Allies, who lost 8,000 dead to 437 British, and established British naval dominance for the next 100 years.

RIGHT: **Victorious British ships around the burning hulk of a French ship during the Battle of Trafalgar.** *Hulton Getty Picture Collection*

INSET, RIGHT: **"The Battle of Trafalgar, 21st October 1805: fall of Nelson." Oil painting by Denis Dighton.** *Hulton Getty Picture Collection*

line, they could destroy a portion of the enemy fleet in detail, as long as their own fleet could close the gap with the enemy. The most vulnerable portion of a sailing warship was the bow and stern, and if a line of warships sailed straight towards an enemy line, the lead warship was exposed to the combined fire of the enemy ships (a situation known as "crossing the T"). It is a testimony to the audacity of Nelson and these other great commanders that they knew when to take that risk. Britain became the dominant seapower in the world during this period, not because her ships were better, but because her admirals knew how to make the best of the tools they were given. It was no surprise that after 1811, British ship designers sought to improve the strength of the bow and stern of ships of the line by curving the forcecastle and the stern, making them less vulnerable to raking shot.

Following 1815, the great era of the great sailing navies came to an end. The last sea battle using ships of the line was Navarino, fought in 1827 between the British, French and Russians on one hand, and the Turks on the other. The Turks proved no match for the combined firepower of the allies. The British naval supremacy created by her sailing fleets had ushered in the "Pax Britannica", where her trade and imperial ambitions reached every corner of the globe. The same period saw the full flowering of the Industrial Revolution, and the emergence of America as an industrial power. This industry and the technological developments it spawned would alter naval warfare forever. The warships of 1827 were similar to those of two centuries before. Within a decade, all existing sailing warships would be considered obsolete, as the era of sail gave way to the age of steam.

Battle of Navarino

The battle of Navarino, 1827, was the last large-scale naval battle fought by wooden-walled sailing ships. During the War of Greek Independence, fought to free Greece from Turkish rule, the major European maritime powers, Britain, France and Russia, demanded an armistice. When the Turks refused, they sent a combined fleet of 11 ships of the line, nine frigates and four smaller ships under the command of Admiral Codrington to assist the Greeks. Turkey had allied with Egypt and in October 1827 an Egyptian-Turkish fleet made up of three ships of the line, 15 frigates and over 50 smaller ships and troop transports, was sent to bring reinforcements to the Turks fighting in Greece. On October 20 the Egyptian-Turkish fleet was at anchor in the harbour in Navarin Bay (now Plyos), off the southwestern Peloponnese, when the British-French-Russian fleet entered the harbor. In the ensuing battle the more technologically advanced guns of Codrington's ships demonstrated their superiority, sinking three-quarters of the bottled-up Egyptian-Turkish fleet and forcing others ashore. There were no losses to the British-French-Russian fleet. The scale of the destruction to the Egyptian-Turkish fleet led to the setting up of an independent Greek state: within a year Egypt left the war and the Turks began their retreat from Greece.

LEFT: **The Spanish three-decker** *Santissima Trinidad* **at the Battle of Trafalgar.** *via Chrysalis Images*

RIGHT: **Navarino was fought on October 20, 1827. Top picture shows Turkish shore battery on the island of Sphakthera in the foreground, and the Greek town of Navarino in the background. The bottom picture view from the south-west shows the curved formation adopted by the Turks, with the Allied fleet of Admiral Codrington on the inside (right) of the arc.** ©*Archivo Iconografico, S.A./CORBIS*

The Dreadnoughts
TRANSITION FROM SAIL TO STEAM

The century which followed the end of the Napoleonic Wars in 1815 saw the transformation of naval warfare. Within a decade, steam propulsion had been introduced and its effectiveness was proven. Half a century later, sailing warships were gone, replaced by a new breed of steam-powered, ironclad men of war, firing rifled shells rather than roundshot. By the start of World War I (1914-18), dreadnought battleships could fire a 12-inch shell a dozen miles with ease, submarines threatened the world's shipping lanes, and mines and torpedoes introduced fresh hidden dangers for the world's navies. Navies struggled to keep up with the changes forced upon it by this technological revolution. For naval commanders, coping with these developments must have been even harder.

Following 1815, the world's navies continued to use wooden warships to form their main battlefleets. These ships increased in size during the early 19th century, and most of these new vessels were First Rates, carrying over 90 guns. Warships became longer, and a new breed of "super-frigates" superseded the 74-gun warships as ships of the line. The term "frigate" even fell into disuse, and was replaced by the term "cruiser," meaning a powerful warship which operated independently from the main battlefleet. In 1809 American engineer Robert Fulton successfully operated the paddlewheel steamer *Phoenix* off the Delaware River. In 1815, the Scottish steamboat *Duke of Argyle* steamed from Glasgow to London, marking the first ocean voyage using steam propulsion. During the next decade, the number of small steamers increased exponentially, as did the reliability of contemporary steam engines, and the size of the vessels.

RIGHT: **The screw steamer USS *Essex*. (1876-1930).** *TRH Pictures/US Navy*

Britain maintained the world's largest navy, but the Admiralty viewed the introduction of steam with suspicion. The first naval steamer was the tender *Comet* (1822), and subsequent vessels served as small auxiliary craft rather than as warships. The Admiralty refused to consider steam-powered warships, and as late as 1835 it commissioned new sailing warships for the fleet. The British were forced to change their position during the 1840s, when the French began converting their battlefleet to steam. These early steam battlefleets could operate under sail or steam; a clutch disengaged the propeller shaft when required, and the screws were raised into a recess in the bottom of the hull to avoid drag when under sail. By the outbreak of the Crimean War (1854-56), both the French and the British fleets contained a core of steam-powered warships of various sizes.

During the Napoleonic era, the size of guns carried on warships increased, but apart from grapeshot (which was fired at close range), all projectiles were solid iron spheres. During the 1840s, the French ordnance designer Henri Paixhans invented a gun that was capable of firing exploding "shells." These projectiles were developed from the hollow, round mortar bomb used since the 17th century, but they used an impact fuse, not one which burned for a set

time. The effectiveness of these shell guns was demonstrated in 1854, when a Russian squadron completely destroyed a fleet of wooden Turkish warships at the Battle of Sinope, in the Black Sea. The technology of naval ordnance had now gained a temporary advantage over the development of warships, and from that point on, all wooden warships were vulnerable. The same conflict saw the development of floating batteries by the French, which they used during the Siege of Sevastopol. Sheathed in wrought-iron plate, these rafts proved impervious to Russian counter-battery fire. For the next 80 years, the development of naval ordnance and warship armor would develop together, with both gun designers and naval engineers striving to regain the brief tactical advantage of one over the other.

Iron was already being used to form the hulls of some merchant vessels, such as the SS *Great Britain*, launched in 1844. The Royal Navy experimented with iron-hulled frigates and troop transports, but it was the French who seized the initiative. In 1859 the steam-powered ironclad warship *Gloire* was commissioned into French service. This revolutionary warship was converted from an older frigate, and her oak hull was strengthened by 4-inch iron plate. Although her small broadside battery of conventional guns were unimpressive and her armor plating only

LEFT AND ABOVE: **Two engravings of operations during the Russo-Turkish War of 1877, including a rather fanciful underwater mining party.** *Chrysalis Images*

covered her main battery (or "casemate"), the British had nothing to match her. Overnight she rendered wooden line-of-battle ships obsolete, and prompted the first naval arms race. Sixteen more French ironclads were commissioned, causing a panic in Britain.

Within a year the Royal Navy responded by commissioning HMS *Warrior*, an even larger ironclad warship, with thicker plating protecting her main battery. Displacing 9,137 tons, her armament was as impressive as her size, making her considerably more powerful than the *Gloire*. Her conventional main armament of smooth-bores was augmented by 11 breech-loading rifled guns, experimental weapons which proved somewhat unreliable. British industrial capacity ensured that the French were left behind, and subsequent ironclads were improvements of the original design. By 1870, the Royal Navy had 25 large ironclad warships, classified as either "cruisers" or "battleships," the new term for ironclad ships of the line.

Across the Atlantic, the outbreak of the American Civil War in 1861 found both sides unprepared for the conflict. The Union possessed a sizeable navy of wooden screw warships, but no ironclads. Prompted by rumors that the Confederates were building an ironclad, the Secretary of the Navy Gideon Welles commissioned Swedish-born designer John Ericsson to construct a small ironclad vessel armed with two guns, mounted in a revolving turret. The result was the USS *Monitor*, which was completed in February 1862. Unlike the *Warrior*, the tiny *Monitor* was completely armored, with her turret sitting on an iron-plated hull which barely rose out of the water. Her engines and magazines were all below the waterline.

In the South, the Confederate Secretary of the Navy Stephen Mallory was well aware of the problems facing his new nation. With no navy to speak of and a long exposed coastline, the Confederates were unable to match the power of the Union Navy. Mallory's solution was to close the gap by relying on technical innovation. By employing armored warships and rifled guns, a handful of ships might be able to challenge the Union's naval blockade of the Confederacy. His favored vessel was a mobile version of the French floating batteries, capable of being produced using the limited shipbuilding facilities available. When

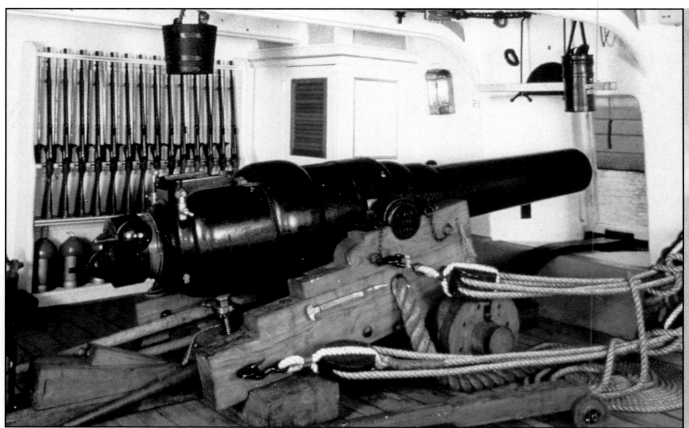

ABOVE: **One of HMS *Warrior*'s breech-loading guns; very different to those seen at Trafalgar, but in fact not particularly successful.** *TRH Pictures*

RIGHT: **USS *Constellation* (1862) one of the wooden screw warships which were rendered obsolete by the introduction of the ironclad.** *TRH Pictures/US Navy*

ABOVE: **USS *Cairo* 1852 photographed on the Mississippi River during the Civil War.** *Chrysalis Images*

Federal troops abandoned the Virginian port of Norfolk, they partially destroyed the wooden steam frigate USS *Merrimack*. Confederate engineers converted the hull into a casemate ironclad by adding an iron-plated casemate over the existing hull. Her armament consisted of 10 guns, a mixture of smooth-bores and rifled weapons.

On March 8, 1862, the *Merrimack* (now re-named the CSS *Virginia*) steamed out of Norfolk into Hampton Roads. In the next four hours she demonstrated the superiority of the shell gun and the resilience of her armor, destroying two Union wooden warships before returning to a hero's welcome. The following morning she tried to complete her destruction, but found herself facing the USS *Monitor*, which had only reached Hampton Roads the night before. In what was the first fight between two ironclads, the *Virginia* and the *Monitor* hammered each other at close range, but failed to damage their opponent. Although the Battle of Hampton Roads was a stalemate, it changed the course of naval warfare forever. Wooden warships were clearly redundant, and the future lay in armor plate and large guns.

Subsequent ironclads produced by both sides were based on their respective prototypes, and all future turret ironclads produced for the US Navy were given the typological name "monitor." Both monitor and casemate ironclads proved their worth, but they were exclusively coastal vessels, smaller than the seagoing ironclads of Britain and France.

In Europe, designers continued to develop new forms of warships, and experimented with revolutionary designs of ships and guns. The Battle of Lissa, fought in 1866 between Italy and Austria-Hungary, was won by the Austrian use of ramming tactics, a throwback to the days of ancient galley warfare. Consequently, for the next decade, naval engineers added rams to the bows of their warships, even though advances in ordnance meant that naval battles could be fought at ever-increasing ranges. This was an era of experimentation, where a constant stream of technical developments leapfrogged over each other. After Lissa, there is no evidence that the ram was used effectively in action.

Another design concept was the use of the armored turret, the use of which was embraced in America. In Britain, its leading advocate was the naval officer Captain Coles, who helped design the Royal Navy's first turreted warship HMS *Captain*. Although this prototype foundered, an improved version was produced in 1871; HMS *Devastation* carried four 12-inch muzzle-loading guns, carried in two armored turrets.

During the Victorian era, the British led the way in experimentation, trying almost every variant of armor,

The Battle of Lissa

The struggle for German unification in the mid-19th century brought the increasingly powerful German state of Prussia into conflict with the historic power, Austria. During the Seven Weeks' War of June-August 1866, the Italians, themselves in process of unifying their country, allied with the Prussians against Austria. Count Carlo di Persano led the Italian fleet across the Adriatic in an assault on the Dalmation island fortress of Lissa. The garrison's defences withstood the attack long enough to enable the Austrian fleet under Wilhelm von Tegetthoff to reach the island on the morning of June 20. Although numerically stronger (the commonly accepted figures are 12 armored and 17 unarmored Italian ships opposed to seven Austrian armored and 11 unarmored ships), the Italian fleet was poorly prepared. Tegetthoff organized his fleet into a wedge-shaped formation and attacked the Austrian line, which was in some confusion as di Persano was in the process of transferring flagships from the *Re d'Italia* to the *Affondatore*. Tegetthoff's ships broke through the Austrian line and in the close-quarter melee that ensued, superior Austrian gunnery began to gain the advantage, setting fire to the Italian ironclad *Palestro*, which later blew up. Both sides, following naval thinking of the time, also attempted to ram opposing ships and the Austrian flagship *Ferdinand Max* was successful in sinking the battleship *Re d'Italia*. Subsequently, the Italian fleet retired to Ancona. Tegetthoff did not pursue. Although Lissa had little effect on the outcome of the war, it was the largest ironclad battle of the 19th century and highlighted the changing nature of naval warfare at the time, as tactics developed to make the most of the new technology of the armored, steam-propeled warships with their increasingly effective armament, through the development of breech-loading guns.

propulsion and guns. This represented the desire to remain ahead of other maritime powers in the technological naval revolution. A rival to the gun turret as a means of gun battery protection was the central battery design, or "armored citadel," where a broadside arrangement gave a restrictive field of fire, but allowed for extensive armored protection. The two systems (with variants) continued to be used until the 1880s, when a revolution in armament made the casemate design impractical.

Until 1880, all but a handful of naval guns were muzzle-loading weapons. The breech-loading Armstrong guns mounted in HMS *Warrior* were not a success, as when they were fired, gas leakage around the breech dramatically reduced the effectiveness of the weapon. While research continued, muzzle-loading weapons were becoming almost unmanageably large. In the 1870s, the Italians equipped their battleship *Duilio* with two turrets, each carrying a 100 ton (17.7-inch) muzzle-loader designed by Armstrong. The British response was immediate, and in 1876 HMS *Inflexible* was commissioned, which carried 80-ton (16-inch) guns. Loading these huge guns caused problems for designers, as the barrels needed to be short. At a time when accuracy and the length of a rifled barrel were closely linked, gun designers were forced to use short barrels in order to facilitate reloading on board ship. Reloading these cumbersome guns was a lengthy process, so warships had a slow rate of fire. It was becoming increasingly obvious that the future lay in using an improved breech-loading design.

The problem with gun design in 1880 was that the science and mathematics of ballistics had overtaken technological development. Designers knew that long, rifled guns capable of firing shells at a high velocity were the most effective weapons in terms of range and accuracy. The breakthrough came when British designers invented a leak-proof breech mechanism, sealing the block to the rear of the barrel through the use of an interrupted screw thread. At the same time, improvements in gun manufacture permitted the production of longer barrels. While earlier barrels were cast in one or more pieces, these new guns were built up by heat-shrinking a series of progressively larger tubes onto each other, or by winding wire around a central core. The introduction of all-steel barrels permitted the creation of longer gun barrels. Velocity was also improved by the development of prism powder, then cordite, a nitro-cellulose propellant which burned slower than black powder, but burned with a greater intensity. This revolutionary breed of long, rifled, breech-loading guns took naval gunnery into a new modern age.

During the bombardment of Alexandria by the British in 1882, the Royal Naval battleships were equipped with large muzzle-loaders. Within five years, these warships had been rendered obsolete. In 1887 the British launched the first in a series of battleships which were designed from the keel up to carry these new naval guns. The first of the "Admiral" class was HMS *Collingwood*, armed with four 13.5-inch (67-ton) breech-loading barbette-mounted guns. Guns of this size could only be mounted in turrets, or their open counterpart, the barbette mount (an open-topped armoured enclosure). From that point on, battleships were larger, better armed and fitted with improved armor and propulsion systems. For the first time, these warships used electrical power for lighting, and by the end of the century, electricity would be used for a variety of functions, including operating the guns, powering searchlights and running auxiliary engines. Using hindsight, naval historians have classified these improved Victorian-era battleships as

Virginia v Monitor

The battle between CSS *Virginia* (formerly USS *Merrimack*) and USS *Monitor* marks the beginning of armored naval warfare. The engagement took place during the American Civil War, in Hampton Roads, Virginia. On March 8, 1862, the steam frigate *Virginia* had sunk two Unionist warships and driven a third ashore, threatening to steam up the Potomac and bombard Washington. *Monitor* arrived the next day, March 9, and although the four-hour battle was inconclusive, *Virginia* was forced to retreat. The era was one in which the leading navies in the world were engaged in an arms race to armor-plate and produce the first iron-hulled warships. Swedish innovator John Ericsson had designed a radically new ship for the US Navy, USS *Monitor*, carrying her two 11-in guns in a revolving 8in-armoured turret which protected the crew from enemy fire and enabled the gun to be fired in any direction, irrespective of the position of the ship. It also had forced air ventilation for the crew below decks. Although *Monitor's* encounter with CSS *Virginia* was inconclusive, the potential of the new design was demonstrated when *Virginia's* cannon shot bounced harmlessly off the armoured turret. This new design rendered the latest ironclad warships obsolete, as their guns could fire only fixed broadsides, and even the British ironclads were protected by only 4.5-in armor plate. Navies began to build their own warships using rotating armored turrets and even developed monitor-type vessels: shallow-draught warships with a large beam capable of carrying one or two large guns for shore bombardment.

FAR LEFT AND LEFT: Virginia v Monitor, the shape of things to come. The engagement between the two ironclads on March 8, 1862, was mostly fought at point-blank range. TRH Pictures/US Navy and TRH Pictures/National Maritime Museum

ABOVE: **USS *Maine* seen entering Havana Harbor, January 25, 1898. She was destroyed by an explosion just over two weeks later.** *via TRH Pictures*

ABOVE LEFT: **Casemate ironclad USS *St. Louis*, flagship of Flag Officer Andrew Hull Foote at the bombardment of Fort Donelson.** *Chrysalis Images*

LEFT: **Union transports at Pittsburg Landing on the Tennessee River. River transportation along the Misssssippi River and its tributaries played a vital part in the ultimate Union victory in the war.** *Chrysalis Images*

"pre-dreadnoughts", whose 20-year reign ended with the creation of HMS *Dreadnought* in 1906. During this period, battleship design centered around achieving the ideal balance of armament, protection and speed. By the 1890s, barbette mounts had been replaced by gun turrets, and the British "Majestic" class of seven pre-dreadnoughts carried an integrated armament of four 12-inch guns in two turrets, broadside batteries of 6-inch secondary guns, and quick-firing weapons designed to counter the threat from light torpedo boats.

In the United States, a resurgence in naval interest was spawned in part by the naval theorist Captain Alfred Mahan (who advocated the pursuit of "seapower"), and by an increasing involvement in the politics of the Americas in line with the policies of the "Monroe Doctrine." The first of these new battleships was the USS *Maine*, whose twin turrets mirrored current designs for coastal defence battleships developed by the British. By 1898, the US Navy had six battleships, and more being built. When the USS *Maine* was destroyed in Havana Harbor in February 1898, America claimed the loss was an act of sabotage by the Spanish, although the real cause has never been proven. The *Maine* disaster led to war between Spain and the United States, and in the one-sided Battle of Santiago (1898), a force of Spanish cruisers were decimated by superior firepower from the American battleships. The effectiveness of contemporary weaponry had been demonstrated.

In 1905, an even more impressive demonstration would force designers to re-evaluate the effectiveness of these pre-dreadnought battleships. In 1904, a war between Russia and Japan found Russia ill-prepared. Her Pacific fleet based at Port Arthur included modern battleships, but they were outnumbered by the equally modern Japanese navy. The Japanese had already decimated an outdated Chinese Imperial fleet at the Battle of the Yalu River (1899), and while the Russian navy was plagued by political unrest and discontent, the Japanese had brought their force to the peak of efficiency. At the indecisive Battle of the Yellow Sea (1904), both sides seemed reluctant to expose their battleships to the risk of attack by torpedo boats, or risk a

full-scale gunnery duel. The Russian fleet remained in port, and called for reinforcements from Europe. A motley collection of modern and obsolete battleships and cruisers was gathered and sailed from Russian Baltic ports to the

LEFT: **USS *Maine* in Havana, February 14, 1898.** *TRH Pictures/US Navy*

BELOW: **The Great White Fleet was the popular name given to the US battle fleet between 1907 and 1909, and was used by President Theodore Roosevelt to demonstrate American naval prowess.** *TRH Pictures/US Navy*

Far East, by way of the Indian Ocean. By the time they reached the war zone, the Russian fleet was destroyed, scuttled to prevent its capture when Port Arthur fell to Japanese troops. Arriving too late to prevent this defeat, the fleet commander, Admiral Rodzhdestvensky decided to restore national prestige by attacking the Japanese fleet. The result was the Battle of Tsushima, fought on May 27, 1905. The Japanese, led by Admiral Togo "crossed the T" of the Russian fleet, and decimated their opponents through superior gunnery. Almost the entire Russian fleet was destroyed, vindicating the belief that ordnance was the key to naval combat. It demonstrated the superiority of the gun over

Battle of Tsushima

The Russo-Japanese war (1904-05) was fought for dominance of the Pacific. In October 1904 the Russian Baltic fleet under the command of Admiral Rozhestvensky embarked from Liepaja (today in Latvia) on a 7,000-mile-long journey to relieve the blockaded Russian fleet at Port Arthur. En route, a major diplomatic incident occurred when the fleet opened fire on British trawlers near Dogger Bank in the North Sea in the mistaken belief they were Japanese torpedo boats. The difficulties of coaling meant that the Russian ships were forced to carry unusually large deck-loads of coal, preventing effective battle practice en route, exacerbating the problems of aged ships and poorly trained crews. By the time Rozhestvensky reached the China Sea, Port Arthur had surrendered to the Japanese and on May 27-28, Admiral Togo achieved a crushing victory against the Russian fleet in the Straits of Tsushima, between Japan and Korea, sinking 29 of the 38 Russian ships engaged. The battle demonstrated the effectiveness of the new breed of fast armored battlecruisers, the Japanese "Tsukuba" class being among the first built in the world. With a top speed of 22kts they had a 6kt advantage over the opposing warships, enabling them to choose their positions, maintaining a consistent target range with their superior 12-inch guns. The battle effectively ended Russian naval aspirations and heralded a new maritime power in the Pacific.

existing warship armor, forcing naval designers to come up with a new form of protection. The result would be the creation of the "dreadnought."

While the main focus of naval development centered around the battleship, its armor and guns, other technological developments forced the navies of the world to embrace new doctrines and ship types as a response. The most revolutionary of these was the development of the submarine. Although underwater warships had been con-

FAR LEFT: **USS *Hunley* at Charleston, SC, December 6, 1863.** *TRH Pictures/US Navy*

LEFT: **Excellent portrait of the second battleship named the USS *Maine*, which was commissioned in 1902, as one of a class of three coastal defence battleships. HMS *Dreadnought* ensured that this pre-dreadnought battleship was obsolete within five years of its launch.** *TRH Pictures*

OVERLEAF: **USS *Iowa* commissioned in 1897. She took a leading part in the Battle of Santiago, July 3, 1898.** *TRH Pictures/US Navy*

templated since the late 18th century (one of the first had been the American *Turtle* of 1775), the first operational submarine was built during the American Civil War. In 1864 the CSS *Hunley* sank the blockading warship USS *Housatonic*, but the submarine foundered during the attack. A Spanish designer developed the idea of a double hull containing a buoyancy tank, and in the late 1870s the British experimented with submarines, the prototypes being named *Resurgeram* and *Resurgeram II*. All these craft were powered by hand cranks, and could only submerge a few feet, and for a few minutes. The Russians and Greeks also experimented with submarine design, but it was the Irish-American designer John P. Holland who first produced a workable submarine after several false starts. The US Navy bought the sixth version of his steam-powered submersible in April 1900, naming it the USS *Holland*. Subsequent improvements produced a small submarine that employed a petrol engine for use on the surface, and an electric motor for running when submerged. The French were also instrumental in the production of working submarines, and by 1905 designer Maxime Laubeuf had produced a boat which could recharge its own batteries while underway, which increased the submarine's operating range. The British Admiralty had been skeptical of submarine designs, and naval officers deemed the craft "unsporting." Despite this opposition, British versions of the Holland boats came into service during the first decade of the 20th century. In Germany, Admiral Tirpitz opposed the introduction of sub-

marines into the service, but partly in response to the launch of HMS *Dreadnought*, *Unterseeboot* 1 (U-1) was built in Kiel during 1906, based on a modified French design. This first "U-Boat" used a paraffin-powered engine, but in 1909 the British introduced the first diesel-powered submarine ("D" class). The Germans developed their own class of boats in response, and from U-19 on, all subsequent German boats were diesel-powered. When World War I began in 1914, the Imperial German Navy had only six diesel-powered U-boats, but another 22 were immediately laid down. Most displaced 1,200 tons, and were capable of top speeds of 17kts on the surface and 7kts submerged. Although unrestricted U-boat warfare was only instituted in 1917, the threat provided by these small craft and their successors had a profound impact on the way naval warfare was conducted. In 1914, submarines were considered something of a novelty. Three years later, they almost brought the world's greatest maritime power to her knees.

ABOVE RIGHT: U35 **running on the surface in the Mediterranean and about to submerge April-May 1917.** *TRH pictures/IWM*

BELOW RIGHT: **HMS** *Verulam* **runs trials in 1918, one of the new "V" and "W" class of destroyers.** *Bison Picture Library*

BELOW: **USS** *Holland*, **SS-1, at the Naval Academy with the class of 1902 aboard. Note ship's bell.** *TRH Pictures/US Navy*

The First Submarine Battle of the Atlantic

As in World War II, the battle for control of the Allies vital transatlantic shipping routes in World War I, fought largely between Allied warships and merchant vessels, and German U-boats, was vital to the eventual outcome in the war. Three times in the war the Germans resorted to unrestricted warfare — the first two campaigns, from February 1915 to September 1915 and from February to April 1916, were abandoned because of fears that they would bring the United States into the war. The third campaign started in February 1917 and continued until the end of the war, the increasingly desperate situation of the blockaded Germans overriding fears of antagonising the U.S. (which declared war April 6, 1917). The attacks by U-boats on shipping reached their peak in April 1917, with 860,000 tons being sunk, but the following month the Allies introduced the convoy system of merchant ships escorted by British and American warships which greatly reduced losses, although the system had been hitherto opposed by the British Admiralty until it was almost too late. Another well-known measure to counter the U-boat threat was the famous Q-ships, warships disguised as merchantmen which lured unsuspecting U-boats to within range of their concealed guns. These had been introduced by the Royal Navy in 1914 but despite some successes, sank only 11 U-boats while losing 27 of their number.

Three views of German U-boats of World War I.

FAR LEFT: **U-boat conning tower.** *Bison Picture Library*

ABOVE LEFT: **Machine room.** *Bison Picture Library*

LEFT: **U-boat torpedo room.** *Bison Picture Library/IWM*

Submarines proved successful mainly because they provided a perfect delivery system for the torpedo. In the 19th century, torpedoes were static, the submerged mines which proved their effectiveness during the American Civil War. While static mines continued to be developed, particularly by the smaller maritime powers, these passive weapons did little to influence warship design and employment. Robert Whitehead pioneered the development of the torpedo as an offensive weapon in 1866. Both mines and torpedoes were designed to destroy warships by blowing a hole in them, but "locomotive torpedoes" could be used selectively, and were therefore seen as "anti-battleship" weapons. Unlike other prototypes, the Whitehead torpedo used compressed air as a propellant and included a hydrostatic control to keep the torpedo submerged after it was fired. By 1900, improvements in warheads and the introduction of fuel to the propellant made the torpedo one of the most formidable weapons in the naval arsenal.

The navies of the late 19th century struggled over the best way to use this new weapon. During the American Civil War, small launches fitted with static "torpedoes"

ABOVE: ***Little David*** **"torpedo boat" with photographer's wagon at Charleston SC, 1864.** *Chrysalis Images*

ABOVE RIGHT: **USS *Casco* in the James River, Va in 1865 while serving as a torpedo vessel. Note the spar torpedo equipment at her bow.** *Chrysalis Images*

RIGHT: **Italian motor launch at Venice during WWI.** *Chrysalis Images*

were used by both sides, and the notion of using small fast craft to bring the torpedo within range of its target was considered the ideal form of delivery system.

The German "torpedo boat" *Zieten* launched in 1875 was typical of dozens of small torpedo-firing vessels being built in Europe and America from the 1870s on. These small, fast craft constituted a new breed of warship; ideal for the hit-and-run tactics which the torpedo attack required, and which existed solely to launch torpedoes at major enemy warships. The idea of small, inexpensive warships which could attack and sink battleships appealed to the world's smaller navies, prompting the British to develop a response. The first "torpedo boat destroyer", HMS *Lightning* was launched in 1876, but the "destroyer" design was perfected during the last decades of the century through the employment of new, quick-firing guns. Their role was to screen the main battlefleet from attack by torpedo boats, but by 1914 torpedoes were also fitted to these craft, and the distinction between torpedo boats and destroyers had become blurred. Both were capable of launching torpedo attacks, as were cruisers. At Queen Victoria's Diamond Jubilee Review of the Fleet in 1897,

ABOVE: **Austro-Hungarian battleship *Szent Istvan* sinking after being after being torpedoed by Italian MTB *MAS15* and *MAS21* off Premuda Island June 10, 1918.** *Bison Picture Library/IWM*

RIGHT: **US Navy crew man the bow deck gun of a transport.** *Bison Picture Library*

ABOVE: **HMS *Furious* started life as a battlecruiser but was converted to an aircraft carrier. Here she is seen with a flight of torpedo-bombers during 1930s.** *US Naval Historical Center via Bison Picture Library*

ABOVE RIGHT and RIGHT: **In 1916, when HMS *Furious* was converted into an aircraft carrier, she retained a rear gun turret until the end of the war. These photographs show her appearance shortly afterward. During 1921 her superstructure was removed, turning her into a fully-fledged fleet carrier.** *Bison Picture Library; Robert Hunt Library via TRH Pictures*

HMS *Turbinia* made her debut, her steam-driven turbine producing speeds in excess of 34kts. From 1900 on, most destroyer engines would use this new form of propulsion.

The introduction of machine guns and recoil systems during the 1880s prompted the development of small naval guns capable of rapid fire. By the end of the century, 3-pounder, 6-pounder and 12-pounder "Quick Fire" (QF) guns were carried on most surface warships, and formed the principal armament of the destroyers. By 1914, QF guns with calibres of up to six inches were fitted onto battleships, cruisers and some destroyers. New fleet tactics were also developed to counter the threat from torpedoes, and cruisers were reincorporated into the main fleets, to provide an inner screen between the battleships and the enemy. For all their romance and dash, destroyers or torpedo boats never constituted a significant challenge to major warships due to the effectiveness of anti-torpedo boat measures. The naval gun remained the principal arbiter of the conventional naval battle until after the Battle of Jutland (1916).

WARSHIPS

In 1909, when Louis Blériot flew across the English Channel in his monoplane, the Germans were already experimenting with naval aviation. Graf von Zeppelin was building lighter-than-air dirigibles, which could be used to scout ahead of the fleet, providing information on the location of enemy warships. The Wright Brothers had offered the British their patents in 1907, but they were declined. The Americans were faster to embrace the possibilities offered, and in 1910 a Curtiss biplane flew off a ramp on the bows of the USS *Birmingham*. Other experiments followed, and in 1911, a successful landing was made on the USS *Pennsylvania*. Naval aviation had been born. A Royal Naval officer flew a "hydroaeroplane" off HMS *Africa* in 1912, and by 1914, seaplanes were employed as scouting aircraft by the navy. When war broke out in 1914, a handful of cross-channel ferries were converted into seaplane carriers, and on Christmas Day, aircraft launched from these ships tried to bomb the German Zeppelin yards at Cuxhaven. Although fog denied the aviators a target, they flew over the German High Seas Fleet, proving the value of reconnaissance aircraft. Impressed with these aircraft, the Admiralty sought ways to employ them in greater numbers.

RIGHT: **A Sopwith 1½ Strutter taking off from a platform over a gun turret on the battlecruiser *Australia*.** *Bison Picture Library*

BELOW: **British naval airship escorting a convoy.** *Bison Picture Library*

The liner *Campania* was converted into the first "aircraft carrier," having a flight deck added, and steam trolleys were used to launch seaplanes. Although the battlecruiser HMS *Furious* was converted into an aircraft carrier for regular aircraft, and aircraft took off successfully, landings often resulted in crashes.

Lessons learned from these early mistakes led to the introduction of arrester wire systems and guided landings, first pioneered by the US Navy before the war. Longer carrier decks were developed, and after the war, dedicated carriers were produced, the first being HMS *Eagle*. These early seaplanes were also spotting aircraft, not warplanes. This changed, and in 1915, a Short biplane was designed to carry a torpedo, creating the world's first torpedo bomber. Other wheeled aircraft were designed to carry light bomb loads. In July 1918 seven Sopwith Camels took off from HMS *Furious* and bombed a Zeppelin airfield at Tonderen, in Belgium. These offensive operations were rare, and the

full potential of naval avition was never realised during the war. At the Battle of Jutland in 1916, the British employed the seaplane carrier HMS *Engadine*, but technical problems prevented her aircraft from operating effectively.

The Germans made limited use of Zeppelins for naval reconnaissance, as the dirigibles were diverted for use as bombers. When the Great War ended in 1918, most naval chiefs thought the aircraft was little more than a novelty. This changed in 1921, when the American advocate of naval aviation Brigadier Billy Mitchell successfully bombed and sank the captured German battleship *Ostfriesland*. It would take another 20 years for the importance of this lesson to be realized.

In 1904, the innovative Admiral "Jackie" Fisher became First Lord of the British Admiralty. He chaired a committee which examined new battleship designs, and as a leading advocate of big guns, he wanted to combine speed and protection with the most powerful armament available. Fisher

LEFT: **A key moment in aviation history, a bomb dropped from an American de Havilland biplane hits the captured German battlefield *Osfriesland* during bombing conducted off Virginia in July 1921. These highly-publicized experiments by Brig. General Billy Mitchell demonstrated the effectiveness of airpower against capital ships** *USAF via Bison Picture Library*

BELOW: **HMS *Invincible* at the battle of the Falklands on August 12, 1914. The light battlecruiser blew up at the Battle of Jutland two years later.** *TRH Pictures*

helped push through a radical design for a "super battle-ship" first proposed by the First Sea Lord himself, together with Naval Construction supervisor W. H. Gard. The result was HMS *Dreadnought*, whose keel was laid down in Portsmouth in October 1904. She was built in a record-breaking four months, and was launched on February 10, 1906. Within a year of being laid down, the *Dreadnought* was in service, ushering in a new era in naval warfare. Like the *Gloire* before her, the *Dreadnought* made everything which preceded her obsolete. The *Dreadnought* displaced 22,000 tons, and her 527 foot-long hull was protected by the latest in steel armored plate, 11-inches thick in a central armored belt, with a four-inch plate at bow and stern. Her main armament consisted of 10 12-inch guns, carried in five twin turrets; three on her centerline, and one on each beam amidships. This configuration allowed for an eight-gun broadside, or six guns to fire fore or aft. These weapons had an effective range of 24,000 yards. Guns of this kind

HMS *Dreadnought*

The brainchild of First Sea Lord, Admiral Fisher, HMS *Dreadnought*, launched in 1906 by the Royal Navy, was the first of its kind in the world. The principle of the new dreadnought type was that the ship would be faster than its enemy, would be armored heavily enough to resist current weapons, and its armament would be heavy enough to penetrate the enemy's armor below the waterline. *Dreadnought's* radical design achieved these objectives, rendering all other existing battleships out-moded. It was the first capital ship to have all of its main armament the same calibre (12in) and the first to be powered by steam turbines, giving her a maximum speed of 21kt. It was also well protected; the hull was extremely strong and turrets and belt had 11in armor, the deck 3in. Although the only one of its class, *Dreadnought* was immediately copied by all the major navies and in the ensuing arms race prior to World War I Britain and Germany laid down a number of dreadnought-type battleships. At the outbreak of war Britain had 22 dreadnoughts in service and 13 under construction; Germany 15 in service and 5 under construction. HMS *Dreadnought* served with the Grand Fleet during World War I (ramming and sinking *U29* in the Pentland Firth, February 1915), apart from a sojourn as flagship of 3rd Battle Squadron from May 1916 to March 1918, and was broken up for scrap in 1920.

Battles of the Coronel and the Falklands

Coronel was the first major naval engagement of World War I. Von Spee's German South East Asia Squadron, consisting of the armored cruisers *Scharnhorst* and *Gneisenau* and the light cruisers *Leipzig*, *Dresden* and *Nürnberg*, was attempting to return to Germany via the southern Pacific and South Atlantic when on November 1, 1914, it encountered off Coronel on the Chilean coast one of the British forces sent to deal with the serious threat von Spee posed. The British commander, Rear-Admiral Craddock, decided to engage Spee's larger force rather than break away but his ships were overwhelmed by superior German gunnery, the two cruisers *Good Hope* and *Monmouth* being lost, and only the light cruiser *Glasgow* and armed merchantman *Otranto* surviving. Craddock himself lost his life in the action. Following news of this defeat the British dispatched more warships to the South Atlantic and five weeks later, on December 8, 1914, Spee was surprised at the Falkland Islands by a force commanded by Admiral Sturdee of the two battlecruisers, *Invincible* and *Inflexible,* and the cruisers *Carnarvon, Cornwall, Kent, Bristol* and *Glasgow.* Spee turned to flee when sighting the British ships at harbor at Port Stanley, but although Sturdee's ships were coaling at the time they managed to raise steam quickly and caught von Spee's force, destroying it with long-range gunnery. *Scharnhorst, Gneisenau, Leipzig* and *Nürnberg* were sunk, and von Spee lost his life; only *Dresden* escaped. None of the British ships suffered serious damage.

were already in service, but the maximum carried on pre-dreadnoughts was four, in two turrets. She was also fitted with secondary batteries, and QF guns to repel destroyers and torpedo boats. An anti-torpedo bulge protected her

ABOVE LEFT: **HMS *Inflexible* (sister-ship of HMS *Invincible*) picking up survivors from the *Gneisenau*, December 8, 1914, after the battle of the Falklands.** *Bison Picture Library*

LEFT: Scharnhorst, Gneisenau, Leipzig, Nürnburg and Dresden **seen off the Chilean coast November 26-29, 1914. All except *Dresden* would be sunk at battle of the Falkland Islands in December 1914. For *Dresden* it was a case of out of the frying pan . . . she escaped but was sunk on March 14, 1915.** *Bison Picture Library*

bilge, and anti-torpedo nets could be strung close to her hull when she lay at anchor. Even more innovative was the *Dreadnought*'s propulsion system; steam turbines, which propelled the huge battleship at speeds of up to 21 knots. Like the USS *Monitor*, The name of this remarkable ship came to represent a ship type, and everything which went before was classified as "pre-dreadnought."

The *Dreadnought* prompted a naval race to build battlefleets of these new dreadnought battleships, as earlier battleships were either withdrawn from service or given less important roles. Britain maintained her lead, and her battlefleet outnumbered those of France and Germany combined. In Germany, Tirpitz ordered two prototype "dreadnoughts" (*Westfalen* and *Nassau*), while in the United States, the *Texas* and *New York* were launched to public fanfare. France, Austria-Hungary and Italy followed suit. By the outbreak of World War I in August 1914, the initial dreadnought design had been improved and enlarged, and gunnery methods had become refined to cope with the challenges imposed by clashes between dreadnought battlefleets.

During this period, Fisher developed another ship type, combining the armament of the dreadnought battleship with the speed of a fast cruiser. The result was the "battlecruiser," the first of which was HMS *Inflexible*, originally classified as a "dreadnought armored cruiser." Following their commissioning in 1907, both Britain and Germany developed larger and more powerful battlecruisers, and HMS *Tiger* (1912) carried eight 13.5-inch guns and displaced 29,700 tons. This power and speed was achieved by sacrificing armoured protection. The performance of these battlecruisers at the Battle of Jutland (1916) demonstrated the inherent problems of battlecruiser design, as two were blown apart by superior German gunnery. As the war progressed, the British developed "super-dreadnoughts"; fast battleships which contained none of the deficiencies in protection found in battlecruisers.

The rival battlefleets of World War I relied on naval gunnery to decide the outcome of a naval engagement. The size and power of a naval gun were irrelevant if the shells were unable to hit the target, so alongside developments in naval guns came improvements in gunnery direction. In 1905, the primary armament of a battleship was rarely fired at ranges exceeding 4,000 yards, about a quarter of maximum range. Fisher encouraged Captain Percy Scott to develop methods of rangefinding and targeting which permitted the firing of repeated long-range salvos at the same target. Optical rangefinders were fitted to most warships, and analog calculators were used to determine the target's course and speed. Similar calculations determined the range and bearing of the ship's guns. Similar research was being conducted simultaneously in Germany and America, and German optical systems were widely regarded as being superior to those of other navies. The superiority of German fire control was clearly demonstrated at the Battle of Jutland, which proved a watershed in naval warfare. Poor communications, leadership and co-ordination deprived the larger British fleet of victory, and the German High Seas Fleet inflicted greater losses in ships and crew on the British than they suffered themselves. Strategically, Jutland ensured that Britain's maritime blockade of Germany remained intact, and that the Germans never tried to repeat their successes. The lessons learned from the engagement influenced warship design, gun and projectile development and propulsion systems. By analyzing the battle, the world's navies were preparing themselves for any clash between fleets of battleships which might take place in the future. The problem was, although few people realized it, the days of the dreadnought were over. During 1917, the development of aircraft carriers and the havoc imposed by unrestricted U-boat warfare suggested alternatives to the use of the "big gun" in naval warfare. The misfortune for most maritime powers is that they were slow to realize the importance of these new innovations.

Jellicoe

Admiral John Rushworth Jellicoe (1859-1935) trained as a gunnery officer in the Royal Navy and was the protégé of Admiral Lord Fisher. Jellicoe became Commander-in-Chief of the British Grand Fleet at the outbreak of World War I, leading it at the Battle of Jutland, May 31-June 1, 1916. This was the only time during the war in which the German High Seas Fleet and the British Grand Fleet clashed, and although the Royal Navy suffered the greater losses and Jellicoe's cautious tactics in not pursuing the German ships more vigorously have been subject to great debate, Jellicoe had always known he was "the man who could lose the war in an afternoon" and the German High Seas Fleet did not seriously threaten the Royal Navy for the rest of the war. Jellicoe became First Sea Lord in December 1916, his tenure coinciding with the huge losses of British shipping to unrestricted German submarine warfare and he was dismissed by Lloyd George in December 1917. Measured in temperament although also regarded by some as stifling initiative through a reluctance to delegate, Jellicoe is often contrasted with the more thrusting Admiral David Beatty who commanded the Battlecruiser Fleet at Jutland and succeeded him as Commander-in-Chief of the Grand Fleet, and there has been long debate about their respective roles at Jutland.

Battle of Jutland

Throughout World War I the British Grand Fleet and the German High Seas Fleet were reluctant to risk losing their naval power in a head-on collision. The British were generally content to blockade Germany but by 1916 Scheer, the new commander of the High Seas Fleet, was attempting to lure out sections of the Grand Fleet to whittle down its superiority. On May 31, the High Seas Fleet left harbor, Vice-Admiral Hipper taking the battlecruisers north toward the Skagerrak and the remainder of the fleet under Scheer covering off the Jutland coast of Denmark. The British, able to intercept German radio although uncertain about the size of the opposing force, sent out Admiral Jellicoe's Grand Fleet and Vice-Admiral Beatty's Battlecruiser Fleet. The German and British fleets first encountered each other at 2pm, on May 31. British destroyers of Beatty's force sighted Hipper's battlecruisers, which turned to draw Beatty toward the main German fleet – "the run to the south" – while at the same time both forces opened fire. Faster and more accurate German gunnery sank HMS *Indefatigable* and HMS *Queen Mary*, and two destroyers were lost on each side. At 16.33 the High Seas Fleet came into view and Beatty turned to draw the Germans towards Jellicoe — "the run to the north." Contact was made at 17.56 and although the fleets did not engage closely the British lost the cruiser *Defence*. However, the superior British forces began to inflict heavy punishment and Scheer maneuvered his forces away. Jellicoe, fearing a torpedo attack, also turned and despite a series of sharp skirmishes in the night, Scheer's forces slipped away. Although British losses at Jutland were heavier (losing 14 ships and suffering 6,945 casualties compared with German losses of 11 warships and 3,058 casualties) and Jellicoe was later criticised for missing an opportunity to destroy the High Seas Fleet, the German navy remained penned in German waters for the remainder of the war.

RIGHT: **Damage to the German battlecruiser *Derflinger* after Jutland.** *TRH Pictures*

OVERLEAF: **USS *Missouri* (BB-11) and USS *Ohio* (BB-12) in the lower chambers, Miraflores Locks, Panama Canal, August 31, 1915. In the distance, USS *Wisconsin* (BB-9).** *US Navy Historical Center*

RIGHT: SS *River Clyde* loaded with troops ashore on the beach at Seda el Bahr, Gallipoli. *Bison Picture Library*

LEFT: The German battleship *Blücher* sinks during the battle of the Dogger Bank, January 24, 1915. *Bison Picture Library*

BELOW LEFT: The German cruiser SMS *Köln*, built to replace her name-sake sunk at Heligoland Bight in 1914. This second *Köln* survived the war only to be scuttled by her own crew while she was interned in Scapa Flow in June 1919. *Bison Picture Library*

Scheer

Admiral Reinhard Karl Scheer (1863-1929) entered the German navy in 1879, rising through the ranks to chief-of-staff of the High Seas Fleet in 1910, then being appointed commander of the German High Seas Fleet early in 1916 during World War I. In the early years of the war, as commander of the Second Battle Squadron at the outbreak of the war and initially when commanding the High Seas Fleet, he attempted to use his fleet to lure out the British Grand Fleet in sections to destroy it piecemeal, using a combination of submarine and aerial attacks, including the first and second unrestricted submarine campaigns against merchant shipping, bombarding British coastal towns and sweeps by the High Seas Fleet. After encountering the might of the Grand Fleet at the Battle of Jutland in 1916 he changed his strategy to concentrate on using U-boats in unrestricted warfare in an attempt to starve Britain of food and supplies. Despite bringing America into the war, by 1918 the U-boat campaign was seen increasingly as Germany's best chance of winning the war and on 11 August 1918 Scheer was appointed head of Seekriegsleitung (SKL), chief of admiralty staff, in charge of organising the whole German naval effort, with licence to concentrate resources on the construction of U-boats. However, the end of the war came before the Scheer Programme could take effect. His final plan to throw his entire naval forces at the Allied fleet (Flottenverstoss), drawn up without the knowledge of Germany's political leaders, was never carried out and indeed was a major factor in the subsequent mutiny in the German navy.

World War II
AIRCRAFT CARRIERS & SUBMARINES

World War I was sometimes referred to as the war to end all wars, and in the period immediately following the Armistice, anyone looking back on the carnage and sacrifice of those years would not have been alone in thinking that conflict on such a scale should never happen again. Nevertheless, there was only a relatively short break of just over 20 years before the world again found itself drawn into a truly global conflict in which seapower was to play a vital, if not defining, part. Among the many causes and factors which had led to the outbreak of war in 1914 was the relentless naval arms race between Britain and Germany. With virtually no element of restraint, these two countries had embarked on ambitious expansion plans as each built more larger and powerful ships than the other and the very existence of the resulting battlefleets made some form of conflict almost inevitable. When peace returned in 1918,

one of the first acts of the victorious powers was to ensure the immobilization of the still powerful German High Seas Fleet. Escorted to the British fleet anchorage in Scapa Flow, these once proud ships were eventually scuttled by their crews in June 1919 in order to prevent them being surrendered under the terms of the Versailles Treaty which was about to be signed. In fact the Treaty went further and laid down severe restrictions on the size and composition of the remaining fleet. Significantly no submarines or aircraft were permitted — an indication of how such weapons were even then seen to be the most potent threats. However, it was not only Germany whose navy was to be limited by treaties as the politicians of all the victorious powers were reluctant to become involved in further expensive arms races and sought to limit future naval construction by means of naval treaties.

These, starting with the 1921 Naval Arms Limitation Conference held in Washington, laid down the basic parameters of all types of warships built almost up to the outbreak of war in 1939. As such, they virtually defined the

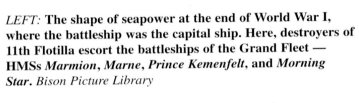

LEFT: **The shape of seapower at the end of World War I, where the battleship was the capital ship. Here, destroyers of 11th Flotilla escort the battleships of the Grand Fleet — HMSs *Marmion*, *Marne*, *Prince Kemenfelt*, and *Morning Star*.** *Bison Picture Library*

BELOW LEFT: **German battleship *Grosse Kurfurst* seen on November 21, 1918, after surrendering at end of World War I.** *Bison Picture Library*

BELOW: ***Hindenburg* scuttled at Scapa Flow; the German High Seas Fleet destroyed itself rather than surrendering under the terms of the Versailles Treaty.** *TRH Pictures/US Navy*

ABOVE: **HMS *Renown* was one of three battlecruisers retained by the Royal Navy after World War I. Of the other two, HMS *Repulse* and the larger HMS *Hood* were sunk. HMS *Renown* survived World War II and was broken up in 1948.** *Bison Picture Library*

ABOVE RIGHT: **HMS *Nelson* was the first new battleship to be built for the Royal Navy after World War I and her design was heavily influenced by the provisions of the 1922 Washington Naval Treaty. She is shown here in 1946 serving as a training ship for the Home Fleet.** *via Leo Marriott*

RIGHT: **One of the most famous British battleships was HMS *Warspite* which fought at the Battle of Jutland in 1916 and subsequently served throughout World War II.** *Bison Picture Library*

size and composition of the fleets that fought all the early campaigns of World War II and it was not until well into the conflict that new ships, freed from artificial constraints concerning size and armament, began to enter service. The Washington Naval Treaty, signed in February 1922, had a number of very significant provisions and foremost amongst these was an agreement that the size of the battlefleets of Britain, the United States and Japan would, in terms of tonnage, be established in the ratio 5:5:3, while those of France and Italy would be proportionately set at 1.75. Other far reaching principles agreed included a 10-year "holiday" on the building of capital ships, a 35,000-ton limitation on the size of battleships and 10,000 tons limit for cruisers. Finally, total tonnage limitations in each class of warship were established and the British and American fleets were permitted a total of approximately 580,000 and 500,000 tons respectively. In order to come within these limits, it was necessary for both to embark on a massive

RIGHT: **The US fleet at anchor off Colon, Panama Canal, in 1933. The US Navy was in transition between the wars. World War II would see the destruction of Britain's once great fleet and by 1945 the US Navy would be the strongest force on the oceans of the world.** *US Navy*

program of scrapping many existing ships, some only a few years old, while many new and larger ships under construction were broken up on the slipways. The Royal Navy scrapped no less than 20 battleships and battlecruisers while the US Navy scrapped 19, although most of these were old pre-dreadnoughts and of virtually no fighting value. Both nations also abandoned massive new capital ships which would have displaced over 50,000 tons in the case of the British "G3" class battlecruisers and almost 45,000 tons in the case of the US "South Dakota" class battleships.

Despite the building holiday, Britain was allowed to proceed with the design and construction of two new 35,000-ton battleships to be armed with 16-inch guns in order to match the two American 32,000-ton "Colorado" class battleships then nearing completion and the two Japanese "Mutsu" class, also armed with 16-inch guns. The British ships, launched in 1925 as the *Nelson* and *Rodney*, thus became the first capital ships of any nation to be built under the limitation of an internationally agreed treaty. The effects of these limitations were immediately apparent in their ungainly appearance caused by the grouping together of the main armament of three triple 16-inch gun turrets on the foredeck where the armor protection could be concentrated, necessitated by the need to keep displacement within the laid down 35,000-ton limit.

As result of the 10-year rule, further new battleships could not be laid down until 1931, but the subsequent 1930 London Naval Treaty led to America, Britain and Japan agreeing to defer any such construction until 1937 although France and Italy were not bound by this arrangement. A second London Treaty was negotiated in 1935, but by 1937 all nations were building new battleships and Japan had completely withdrawn from all treaty restrictions. Although Germany had not been represented at the various Treaty negotiations due to the Versailles restrictions, in 1935 Britain negotiated a separate treaty which restricted the size of the German Navy to 35% of that of the Royal Navy. Finally, in 1938, the original participants in the London Treaty negotiations, apart from Japan, agreed that the limit on capital ship displacement be raised to 45,000 tons and that they could be armed with 16-inch guns. This was despite earlier British efforts to have the 14-inch gun adopted as the maximum permitted.

While all these complex negotiations took place, the German Kriegsmarine managed to surprise and shock the

ABOVE: **The Japanese battleship *Ise* was built in 1916. She is seen here off Sata Point on August 24, 1943, following conversion to hybrid aicraft carrier.** *US Navy Historical Center*

ABOVE LEFT: **Japanese submarine *I-69* was launched in 1934 and is seen here just before the war.** *US Navy Historical Center*

LEFT: **The Japanese heavy cruiser *Ashigara* was launched in 1928.** *TRH Pictures*

rest of the world by building the first of three armored ships, or *Panzerschiffe*, to give them their correct designation. Under the 1919 Treaty of Versailles they had been permitted to replace the old 10,000-ton pre-dreadnought battleships after a period of 10 years. So, in 1929 the first new ship was laid down, its specification stating that it would remain within the stipulated 10,000 tons and would be armed with 11-inch guns, again corresponding to the older ships. However when she commissioned in 1933 as the *Deutschland*, it was immediately apparent that the German naval staff had come up with an ingenious design which, while remaining within the treaty limitations, was actually a completely new type of warship which the contemporary press immediately labeled a "pocket battleship." Within a nominal 10,000 tons displacement (the actual standard displacement was nearer 12,000 tons), the ship carried six 11-inch guns in two triple turrets and also a powerful secondary battery of 5.9-inch and 3.5-inch guns, as well as mounting 21-inch torpedo tubes and carrying two seaplanes. Armor protection was light by capital ship standards, but this saved weight and the use of diesel machinery

109

gave a speed of 26 knots. More significant was the result-ing unrefueled range of 10,000 miles which clearly indicated the main role intended for these ships — commerce raiding on the world's oceans. As such these ships were almost impossible to counter at that time as they outgunned any cruiser which could catch them, and could outrun virtually every other major capital ship.

Almost as a direct result of the appearance of the German pocket battleships, France laid down two 26,000-ton battlecruisers in 1932 and 1934, *Dunkerque* and *Strasbourg*. These carried eight 13-inch guns in two quadruple turrets forward, the overall arrangement owing something to the earlier British "Nelson" class, although a more balanced profile was achieved. Subsequently France laid down two more slightly larger battleships in 1935 and 1935, *Richelieu* and *Jean Bart*. These were of similar design to the "Dunkerque" class but displaced the full 35,000 tons allowed by the Washington Naval Treaty and were armed with 15-inch guns.

France's rival as a Mediterranean naval power was Italy and under the direction of the dictator Mussolini she was determined not to be outdone. Like the French, the Italian Government had not accepted the provisions of the 1930 London treaty and therefore laid down two "Littorio" class battleships in 1934. Armed with nine 15-inch guns they were nominally within the 35,000-ton limit but in war trim standard displacement was eventually in excess of 40,000 tons. They were handsome and powerful ships and a further two were laid down in 1938, although one of these was never completed. Both French and Italian ships were designed for speeds of 30 knots which was now regarded as the standard for major capital ships.

In the meantime Germany had not been idle. Following the successful introduction of the pocket battleship, two more were completed but construction of a fourth was can-celled in favor of a new 26,000 battlecruiser design, of which two were laid down in 1934 and 1935 respectively. These were the *Scharnhorst* and *Gneisenau* armed with nine 11-inch guns in three triple turrets. Substantial sec-ondary and anti-aircraft batteries were also shipped and there was provision for no less than four aircraft. In size and concept they were very similar to the French "Dunkerque" class although, as with many Axis warships, the actual dis-placement was much greater than the announced figure and in this case it was around 32,000 tons. In 1936 Germany

RIGHT: **The after triple 11-inch gun turret of the German battlecruiser *Gneisenau*. A catapult carrying an Arado Ar196 floatplane is mounted on the turret roof.**
Bison Picture Library

FAR RIGHT: **The German battleship *Bismarck* viewed from the quarterdeck of the cruiser *Prinz Eugen* as they prepare for their Atlantic foray in 1941.** *Bison Picture Library*

Bismarck

On May 18, 1941, the German battleship *Bismarck*, accompanied by the battlecruiser *Prinz Eugen*, set sail from the Baltic to attack Allied shipping in the Atlantic. The operation, codenamed "Regenbogen" (rainbow), was under the command of Vice-Admiral Günther Lütjens and was to be the first combat use of the mighty new battleship *Bismarck*. Intelligence reports and aerial reconnaissance alerted the British Admiralty to the danger and Admiral Tovey, Commander-in-Chief of the Home Fleet, stepped up patrols of the escape routes into the Atlantic. On May 23 the British cruisers *Suffolk* and *Norfolk* sighted the German ships between Iceland and Greenland and began shadowing them. Early the next morning *Bismarck* and *Prinz Eugen* were engaged by two ships of Vice-Admiral Holland's Battlecruiser Force. In the brief battle the battlecruiser *Hood* was blown up and sunk with the loss of all but three of her crew of 1,418 and the battleship *Prince of Wales* was also forced to retire. *Bismarck* had not escaped unscathed, either, and loss of fuel forced her to separate from *Prinz Eugen* and head for refuge in Brest. Over the next days she was picked up and lost several times by aerial reconnaissance before Swordfish launched from the carrier *Ark Royal* managed to disable her with a torpedo strike on the evening of May 26. Overnight *Bismarck* was attacked by destroyers and on the morning of the 27th the battleships *King George V* and *Rodney* joined battle, finally sinking the *Bismarck* with the loss of all but about 120 of her crew of 2,400.

laid down two battleships which were to become the *Bismarck* and *Tirpitz*. Armed with eight 15-inch guns on an announced displacement of 35,000 tons they appeared to conform with the Washington treaty and also to the Anglo-German treaty of 1935. In fact, as is now well known, they were considerably larger and the final displacement was in excess of 50,000 tons at full load. Secondary armament comprised 12 5.9-inch guns disposed in twin turrets and a very heavy AAA armament (for that time) of no less than

eight twin 4.1-inch high angle AAA guns backed up by a sophisticated fire control system.

Thus by 1937 two of the future Axis powers in World War II were busily engaged in the construction of new and powerful capital ships although, curiously, the Japanese had made no attempt to enter the race despite having withdrawn from the 1935 London Naval Conference and were not therefore bound by the requirement to defer new construction until 1937. However when they did finally go ahead in that year, they did so in no uncertain style, laying down two monster 64,000-ton battleships armed with nine 18.1-inch guns in three triple turrets backed up by 12 6.1-inch and 12 5-inch dual purpose guns. During World War II this armament was boosted by the addition of around 100 light AAA guns while *Yamato*'s AAA battery eventually included no less than 24 5-inch guns. Due to Japan's island geography and effective exclusion of foreigners, details of these ships only became slowly available to the allied powers after the outbreak of war.

LEFT: **From closest to the camera, Japanese battleships** *Nagato, Kirishima, Ise, Hiuga.* *TRH Pictures/US Navy*

BELOW: **The Japanese 64,000-ton battleship** *Yamato* **was armed with nine 18-inch guns; together with her sister-ship** *Musashi,* **they were the largest battleships ever built.** *TRH Pictures*

All this construction activity could not be ignored by Britain and America and as soon as they were permitted under the terms of the 1930 London Treaty, they began laying down new battleships. In fact Britain began with almost indecent haste, officially commencing work on two new "King George V" class battleships on January 2, 1937, and by the end of that year had no less than five under construction. In practice some preliminary work had already been started prior to that date, including the manufacture of the all important main armament guns and their mountings. The choice of the 14-inch gun was the result of attempts by the British Government at the 1935 London Naval Conference to have this adopted as the limit for subsequent battleship construction. This was actually accepted, but there was a proviso that if the Japanese did not ratify the treaty by April 1, 1937, then the upper limit would revert to the previous 16-inch size. This duly came about, but by then Britain had already begun construction of the ships and their armament in order that they would be ready for any outbreak of hostilities, an occurrence which was now becoming alarmingly likely within a relatively short time. The five "King George V" class were built strictly to the 35,00-ton limit, and for this reason the main armament comprised only 10 14-inch guns in two quadruple and one twin turret, instead of the original intention to carry 12 guns in three turrets. However, in contrast to the French, Italian and German ships (as well as previous British practice) the use of separate batteries of low angle guns for defense

against small surface ships and high angle guns for AAA defense was abandoned in favor of a single battery of 16 dual purpose 5.25-inch guns. These were supplemented by four eight-barreled two-pounder AAA mountings, otherwise referred to as "Chicago pianos." Although thinking along the right lines, the Royal Navy was unfortunate in the choice of the standard Vickers two-pounder, a weapon of limited effectiveness and much inferior to the Swedish Bofors 40mm gun, which was eventually widely used by all the allied navies.

Britain also planned four "Lion" class battleships to be armed with nine 16-inch guns, and these were actually laid down in 1939 but they were scrapped in 1940 before much work had been done. The Royal Navy's last battleship was to be HMS *Vanguard*, which was based on the "Lion" class design but was armed with eight 15-inch guns salvaged from the World War I battlecruisers *Glorious* and *Courageous*. Despite this expedient, the ship did not com-

BELOW: **A view taken aboard the British battleship HMS *King George V* showing the eight-barreled two-pounder pom-pom mountings intended to provide close-range defense against air attack.** *Bison Picture Library*

BELOW RIGHT: **The aircraft carrier HMS *Courageous* was one of three sister ships originally launched in 1916 as battlecruisers, but subsequently converted to aircraft carriers. She is shown here in 1930 with the destroyer HMS *Westminster* in the foreground.** *Bison Picture Library*

mission until 1946, well after the end of hostilities and she was eventually scrapped in 1960.

The United States at this time was determined to keep out of any potential European war but was concerned about Japanese expansionism. Work, therefore, began on two "North Carolina" class battleships in October 1937 and June 1938. The slight delay in starting this program allowed the inclusion of the 16-inch gun in the design of these 35,000-ton fast battleships, which were probably the best all-round examples of their type to see action in World War II. The standard Mk 6 16-inch gun was a reliable and effective weapon which could fire a 2,700lb shell to a range of 36,900 yards. By comparison, the British 14-inch gun fired a smaller 1,600-pound projectile to a greater range of 38,500 yards.

Although the armed forces of the United States made a magnificent contribution to the allied war effort, it is difficult to avoid the conclusion that the greatest asset of the New World was its industrial might — the "Arsenal of Democracy," as it was termed by Franklin Roosevelt. The effects of this are no more apparent than in the massive shipbuilding program undertaken both before and during World War II. To consider battleships only, the two "North Carolina" class were followed by five "South Dakota" class (basically similar but with hull length reduced by 50 feet to conserve the requirement for armour plating) laid down in 1939-40 Subsequently six of the magnificent 33-knot, 45,000-ton "Iowa" class battleships were laid down in

1940-41, and four were completed in good time to see action. In addition, three battlecruisers were also started in 1941-42 of which two were completed and there were even plans to build up to five 60,000-ton "Montana" class battleships to be armed with 12 16-inch guns although these were never laid down and were canceled in 1943. No other nation came near this sort of program at the time.

Despite these massive and expensive construction programs, the days of the battleship were drawing inexorably to a close, although only a few far-sighted individuals realized it at the time. By 1918 Great Britain had successfully pioneered the concept of launching and retrieving aircraft from specially adapted ships and already had the world's first flush-decked aircraft carrier, HMS *Argus*, a converted liner, in service.

Subsequently the battlecruisers *Courageous*, *Glorious* and *Furious* were converted to carriers capable of accommodating up to 48 aircraft after being made redundant by the Washington Treaty provisions. In addition, a battleship under construction in British yards for Chile was purchased in 1917 for conversion to an aircraft carrier and was completed as such in 1923 as HMS *Eagle*. Finally, in 1918, the first vessel ever to be designed from the start as an aircraft carrier was laid down at Armstrong's yard on the banks of the River Tyne and commissioned as HMS *Hermes* in 1924.

Thus, by the mid-1920s Britain had no less six aircraft carriers available. At that time Japan had only the *Hosho*, a light carrier completed in 1922, and America had the USS

Langley, a converted collier. Unfortunately, Britain's commanding lead in ships was offset by the fact that the Navy had lost organic control of its naval aircraft, the former Royal Navy Air Service having been combined with the Army's Royal Flying Corps to form the Royal Air Force (RAF) in 1918. From that date until 1939, when naval aviation finally returned to Admiralty control, all carrie- based aircraft were flown by the Fleet Air Arm of the RAF. While there is no suggestion that the RAF deliberately suppressed naval aviation, neither did it give the wholehearted priority which was required, and consequently by 1939 the aircraft operating from British carriers were substantially inferior to their foreign contemporaries. Even when the Navy finally regained control in 1939, it then lacked the necessary expertise to fully develop appropriate tactics and aircraft. It was not until almost the end of World War II that the British carrier force could operate with anything like the efficiency of its American cousins.

As the threat of war loomed in the 1930s, Britain's naval rearmament began to accelerate and an early project was the laying down of the 22,000-ton aircraft carrier *Ark Royal* which was completed in 1938 and was capable of carrying up to 72 aircraft. Unfortunately, due to the sorry state of the Fleet Air Arm, this number of aircraft was never available, and during World War II the maximum number embarked operationally rarely exceeded 50. She was followed by four

ABOVE: **HMS *Eagle* was converted from the Chilean battleship *Almirante Cochrane* and was unique among British carriers in having two funnels.** *via Leo Marriott*

ABOVE RIGHT: **HMS *Illustrious* was the first of the new British fleet carriers to be completed at the start of World War II. This photo was taken in 1940, shortly after she commissioned.** *Bison Picture Library*

RIGHT: **HMS *Illustrious* lived up to her name during World War II. It was from this ship that the successful raid on the Italian fleet at Taranto was launched.** *via Leo Marriott*

"Illustrious" class carriers of which the first three commissioned in 1940-41 and the slightly modified "Indomitable" also followed in 1941. Initially these were designed to operate 36 or 48 aircraft, although wartime modifications eventually boosted this to 54. Although similar in size to the earlier *Ark Royal,* the smaller aircraft complement was explained by the fact that these ships were the first carriers to incorporate an armored flightdeck, an innovation which saved them from being sunk in action on more than one occasion. The *Illustrious* was heavily hit by German dive-bombers in the Mediterranean in June 1941 and was out of action for over a year while both *Formidable* and *Indomitable* were hit by kamikaze attacks in the Pacific in 1945. The latter were only briefly out of action before

RIGHT: The British fleet carriers completed during World War II were equipped with armored flightdecks. This is HMS *Indomitable*, the fourth in the series. Note the disruptive camouflage pattern. *via Leo Marriott*

BELOW: HMS *Ark Royal* was Britain's first modern large aircraft carrier. Completed in 1938, she could embark up to 72 aircraft and saw considerable action before being torpedoed by a U-boat in the Mediterranean at the end of 1941. *Bison Picture Library*

resuming flying operations and remaining on station. Two further carriers, *Implacable* and *Indefatigable* were commissioned in 1944, and could initially operate 54 aircraft (later raised to 81), this increase being due to the incorporation of a two-deck hangar.

Apart from Britain no other European navy had an operational aircraft carrier in World War II, although the French navy did use the *Béarn*, converted from an uncompleted battleship hull and commissioned in 1927, as an aircraft ferry and training ship. Germany launched the 28,000-ton *Graf Zeppelin* in 1938 but she was never completed while Italy produced the *Aquila*, a converted liner, which was almost complete at the time of the Italian surrender in 1943. She was subsequently damaged by air and underwater attacks and never commissioned. Consequently, although the British carriers were hard pressed and involved in numerous wartime operations in European waters from the Arctic to the Mediterranean, they were never involved in the great set-piece carrier battles which took place in the Pacific between the American and Japanese navies.

Unlike the British situation, the US Navy had retained its own air arm, and in the late 1920s it commissioned two massive 35,000-ton carriers. These were the famous *Lexington* and *Saratoga* which had originally been laid down as battlecruisers in 1921 but whose completion as such was stopped by the tonnage limitations imposed by the

BELOW: **HMS *Venerable* was one of several light fleet carriers laid down for the Royal Navy in 1942-43, although only a few had been commissioned by the end of the war. Built to merchant ship standards and powered by standard destroyer machinery, they proved very versatile in the postwar years and remained in service for several decades.** *via Leo Marriott*

RIGHT: **The escort carrier was originally developed by the Royal Navy to provide air support for North Atlantic convoys. HMS *Campania* was one of the few actually built in British shipyards as American production supplied no fewer than 40 escort carriers during World War II.** *via Leo Marriott*

BELOW: **One priceless asset of the British carriers was their armored flightdeck. Here the crew of HMS *Formidable* begin to clear the wreckage of a Japanese kamikaze. Within hours the ship was operating aircraft again, while a similar attack on an unarmored US carrier would have put it out of action for months.** *Bison Picture Library*

2977

1922 Washington Treaty. However the Navy took advantage of the situation to complete them as aircraft carriers and they entered service in 1927. These imposing ships were characterized by a single massive funnel, which was separated from the main island superstructure, and the cavernous hangars and large flightdeck enabled them to operate up to 80 aircraft. In terms of displacement, they remained the largest carriers ever built until overtaken by the "Midway" class, which was not completed until the end of World War II. In the 1930s America continued a steady program of carrier construction, starting with the 14,500-ton *Ranger* which was completed in 1934. This was the US Navy's first purpose-designed carrier, and it could carry up to 76 aircraft despite being less than half the *Lexington*'s displacement. She was followed by *Yorktown* and *Enterprise* which could operate around 80 aircraft on a displacement of 20,000 tons and the smaller 14,500-ton USS *Wasp* which, despite reduction in size due to treaty tonnage limitations, could still operate the same number of aircraft.

LEFT: **Dauntless dive-bombers ranged on the fore deck of the USS *Enterprise* shortly after Pearl Harbor. Right in the bows are few Wildcat fighters. These aircraft bore the brunt of the early fighting in the Pacific until replace by later types such as the Hellcat, Avenger and Helldiver.**
Bison Picture Library

BELOW: **The USS *Yorktown* as completed in 1937. This ship played a vital part in the Battle of Midway but was then put out of action by Japanese dive-bombers. She was torpedoed and sunk two days later by submarine *I-168*.**
Bison Picture Library

The last prewar carrier to commission was the *Hornet*, which was basically a repeat of the *Yorktown* and was laid down after the treaty restrictions had expired. These ships bore the brunt of action during the 12 months following the attack on Pearl Harbor. While *Ranger* was deployed in the Atlantic and was eventually relegated to training duties, the *Yorktown* was sunk at Midway in June 1942, *Wasp* was torpedoed and sunk south of Guadalcanal in September 1942, and *Hornet* was lost to air attacks at the Battle of Santa Cruz in the following month. Coupled with the earlier loss of the *Lexington*, and the fact that *Enterprise* and *Saratoga* were both seriously damaged, the US Navy was temprarliy without a major fleet carrier in the Pacific by the end of 1942. To help hold the line until the new ships carriers could be built, the British carrier *Victorious* was sent to the Pacific early in 1943.

By 1941, the war in Europe had been raging for almost two years and hostilities with Japan were becoming ever more likely. With all naval treaty restrictions now no longer applicable, the US Navy was able to start construction of a new class of large carriers which would ultimately form the core of the greatest naval task forces ever seen in action. The first of the new 27,000-ton "Essex" class carriers was laid down in April 1941 and commissioned in December 1942, a remarkably short construction time for such a large and complex ship. A further 16 were completed before the end of World War II while a total of 24 were eventually built. The nominal capacity of these ships was 80 aircraft, more or less the same as the preceding classes, but these figures disguised the fact that the "Essex" class would be able to operate the larger and heavier naval aircraft which were then about to enter service. Indeed, with

modifications, some remained operational well into the late 1970s and could cope with modern jet fighters and attack aircraft. Unlike the contemporary British carriers, they were not equipped with armored flightdecks and consequently several where seriously damaged and put out of action for considerable periods when subjected to attack by Japanese kamikaze aircraft although none were actually sunk.

While the "Essex" class was under construction, a potential shortage of carriers had already been anticipated and an emergency program was instituted in 1941 to convert several "Cleveland" class cruiser hulls, then building, to light aircraft carriers. The original hull and machinery was retained, a hangar deck was built onto the hull and this was the covered by a narrow flightdeck. Funnel uptakes were angled to starboard and a small island superstructure was mounted forward of these. The resulting "Independence" class eventually numbered some nine ships and, crucially, all commissioned before the end of 1943. The design was obviously something of a

RIGHT: **USS *Downes* at left and USS *Cassin* at right, USS *Pennsylvania* at rear.** *National Archives.*

BELOW: **USS *Nevada* (battleship) and destroyer *Shaw* burn following the attack. Shortly after this photo was taken *Nevada* was run aground to stop her blocking the main channel.** *National Archives*

Pearl Harbor

On December 7, 1941, Japan declared war on the United States with an aerial attack on the US Pacific Fleet at its main harbor on the Hawaiian island of Oahu. Fearing the immense industrial might of the United States, the Commander-in-Chief of the Japanese Fleet, Admiral Yamamoto, attempted to knock the Americans out of the war with one blow. The air attack, launched from six aircraft carriers, was intended to come (just) after the official declaration of war but as this had been delayed the attack came completely without warning. Out of the 183 aircraft used, the Japanese lost 27. The US Pacific Fleet was devastated. The battleships *Arizona* and *Oklahoma* were sunk, and *California*, *West Virginia*, *Pennsylvania*, *Tennessee*, *Nevada* and *Maryland* were all damaged. Three cruisers and three destroyers were also hit, 188 aircraft destroyed, 2,402 US servicemen and civilians killed and 1,104 wounded. However, the three US carriers *Enterprise*, *Lexington* and *Saratoga* escaped, being at sea at the time, and the Japanese commander of the operation, Vice-Admiral Chuichi Nagumo, cancelled a second air strike which was intended to destroy the huge oil depot at the harbor. Although the Japanese were to dominate the Pacific for the next six months, most of the damaged ships were rebuilt and the Americans were able to recover in time to thwart Yamamoto's attempt to win the decisive Battle of Midway in June 1942.

Yamamoto

The dominant figure in the Imperial Japanese Navy in World War II was Fleet-Admiral Isoraku Yamamoto (1884-1943). His long career in the navy had started at the turn of the century — he was wounded at the Battle of Tsushima in 1905 — and he oversaw the rise of Japan into one of the world's major naval powers by the outbreak of World War II. He was an early advocate of naval air power, being instrumental in building up Japan's carrier fleet, and when Japan decided to go to war in late 1941, he used this air power in a preemptive strike by his fleet on the Americans. His attack on the US naval base at Pearl Harbor in December 1941 devastated the US Pacific Fleet, but did not completely destroy it as the oil storage containers survived and the aircraft carriers were not in port. For the first six months of the war, Yamamoto's Japanese navy had a string of successes in the Pacific, including the Battle of the Java Sea against a combined British, Dutch and US force in February 1942, but Yamamoto realised that the America's huge resources meant that Japan's best hope of victory in the war was to deliver a quick knock-out blow to the US forces. The Battle of Midway in 1942 was devised to destroy the US carrier fleet, but Yamamoto's complex plan failed and Japan suffered its first naval defeat of the war. After Midway, Yamamoto stayed on to command the Japanese navy in the campaign in the Solomon Islands and in April 1943 he was killed when the aircraft he was flying in was shot down. He was given a state funeral.

compromise and only 30 aircraft could be carried for operational purposes, although when employed in the aircraft ferry role, the could stow up 100. Their great virtue was a speed of 32 knots which allowed them to take their place in the fast carrier task groups formed in the latter stages of the Pacific war.

The last major US carriers laid down in World War II were the three "Midway" class which now followed British practice with significant armor protection to both the hull and flightdeck. On a full load displacement of around 60,000 tons, the "Midway" class would be capable of carrying up to 137 aircraft but, although work began in 1943, none of the three laid down were to be in service before the end of the war and their subsequent story belongs to the postwar period.

As wartime experience repeatedly demonstrated, the presence of naval air support was becoming an essential part of any naval operation. While the major fleet actions and massive amphibious operations stole the limelight, the equally vital but less glamorous task of escorting ships carrying men and vital supplies (particularly the North Atlantic) also needed assistance. The British led the way by converting merchant ships to carry a single catapult launched fighter, and later improved on the concept by adding a small flightdeck and hangar. The first complete conversion was HMS *Audacity* that utilized a captured German liner. Although only able to carry a few Wildcat fighters, she nevertheless proved the effectiveness of the concept before being torpedoed and sunk at the end of 1941. By that time other similar conversions were being built in America for both the US and Royal Navies. Eventually over 100 escort carriers (CVE) were built in American yards of which at least 39 were transferred to Britain. The ultimate development of this concept, the "Casablanca" class laid down in 1943-44, could operate up to 34 aircraft, although with a speed of only 19 knots they were not suitable for major fleet actions and were usually employed as escorts and support for amphibious task forces, and for training purposes.

Of all the world's navies, it was perhaps the Japanese who most wholeheartedly embraced the concept of carrier air power at a time when others, while recognizing the potential of the new weapon, were reluctant to see it totally replace the battleship as the main arbiter of seapower. In 1919 they laid down a small 7,500-ton carrier, the *Hosho*,

ABOVE RIGHT: **Three US battleships burn in Pearl Harbor: *West Virginia, Tennessee* (both damaged) and *Arizona* (sunk).** *National Archives*

RIGHT: **The "Essex" class carriers enabled the US Navy to launch its island-hopping campaign against the Japanese from 1943 onward. Photo shows USS *Kearsage*, one of the later "Essex" class which was not completeed until 1946.** *TRH Pictures*

Naval Aviation

The combination of air and sea power as a powerful extension of naval forces came of age in World War II. The greater range of aircraft, and the speed and flexibility with which an area could be encompassed, meant that the aircraft carrier took over from the battleship as the most effective capital vessel of its time, its air group capable of reconnaissance, air defense and direct attack. The extensive use of carriers in the Pacific theater of war meant that air power could be used effectively without having to control land airfields and in the Atlantic carrier-based air cover again was vital in combating the U-boat threat. Battles such as Midway (1942) and the Philippine Sea (1944) were fought without the opposing fleets ever sighting each other. The developments in aviation technology by Japan, USA and Britain during the war were rapid. HMS *Ark Royal*, Britain's newest aircraft carrier at the outbreak of the war, carried 60 Fairey Swordfish biplane aircraft with a maximum speed, when armed with a torpedo, of 110mph. By the end of the war in 1945 aircraft ranged from the agile single-seat Japanese A6M Zero monoplane fighter (preeminent at the start of the war) and Mitsubishi G4M twin-engine bomber to a wide range of US-built equivalents, such as the F6F Hellcat (top speed 380mph), the SBD Dauntless (which sank more warship tonnage than any other aircraft during the war) and SB2C Helldiver dive-bombers and the TBM Avenger torpedo-bomber, as well as larger bombers such as the B-25 used to attack mainland Japan, most famously in the Doolittle Raid on April 18, 1942. Many aircraft, such as the F4U Corsair, were used by the British Fleet Air Arm as well as the US Navy and Marine Corps for ground-attack.

ABOVE: A dramatic shot taken aboard the USS *Enterprise* during the assault on Tarawa in November 1943. A deck crewman makes a brave attempt to rescue the pilot of a Grumman Hellcat which has run off the deck on landing. *Bison Picture Library*

LEFT: The Vought OSU-3 Kingfisher was a reconnaissance seaplane carried by US battleships and cruisers from 1941 onwards although the older Curtiss SOC-4 Seagull biplane also remained in service until 1944. *Bison Picture Library*

FAR LEFT: British naval aircraft generally lagged behind their US and Japanese counterparts in terms of performance. The standard strike aircraft until well into the war was the obsolescent Swordfish biplane, several of which are shown ranged on the deck of HMS *Victorious* in May 1941 prior to making an unsuccessful attack on the German battleship *Bismarck*. *Bison Picture Library*

which is often cited as the world's first purpose-designed carrier. However, although it was certainly the first such vessel to commission (1922), design was heavily influenced by that of the British HMS *Hermes* which was laid down a year earlier. Subsequently, Japan followed British and American practice by converting two redundant battlecruiser hulls. The first of these, *Akagi*, commissioned in 1927 but the second was destroyed by an earthquake while under construction. Consequently a further project was centred around the *Kaga* which had originally been laid down as a 40,000-ton battleship and she was subsequently completed as a 30,000-ton aircraft carrier in 1928. Both the *Kaga* and *Akagi* could carry up to 60 aircraft, but tactical combination was difficult due to the fact that *Kaga* was only capable of 27 knots while the battlecruiser-based *Akagi* could make 32 knots. Japan's next carrier was the relatively small 8,000-ton *Ryujo* which was completed in 1933

LEFT: **The CAM Ship (Catapult Armed Merchantman) was a desperate measure to provide some form of air cover to North Atlantic convoys. Introduced in early 1941, they carried a single Hawker Hurricane fighter which had to ditch in the sea after completing its mission.**
Bison Picture Library

BELOW: **HMS *Audacity* was the first true escort carrier and was converted from a captured German liner, the *Hannover*. Her active career was short but, before being sunk in 1941, she had proved the operational value of the concept of providing close air support to convoys.** *Bison Picture Library*

and was nominally capable of operating up to 48 aircraft but the design was unsatisfactory and a typical wartime complement was only 33 aircraft. The size was deliberately kept below 10,000 tons so that it was not included in the Japan's total carrier tonnage which was restricted by the Washington treaty.

By 1932, when the next pair of carriers was ordered, Japan had effectively decided to abrogate the treaty agreements and subsequently laid down the 16,000-ton *Soryu* and *Hiryu*, which commissioned in 1937 and 1939 respectively. Two more much larger carriers, *Shokaku* and *Zuikaku*, were subsequently completed by September 1941 and these could operate up to 84 aircraft on a standard displacement of 25,600 tons. They were fast and well armored and were perhaps the most successful of the Japanese carrier designs. While these conventional carrier programs were underway, Japan also hedged her bets to some extent by laying down a series of vessels which could be easily adapted for differing roles as required by events. A typical example was the "Chitose" class which were two laid down as 11,000 ton seaplane tenders but could also be converted to fleet oilers or submarine depot ships. There was also provision for them to be converted to aircraft carriers by the addition of a full length flightdeck. These and the similar "Shoho" class could carry only 24-30 aircraft and all four were lost in action.

The Japanese never managed to concentrate on a single basic carrier design such as the American "Essex" class and the wartime construction program was based on the need to

LEFT: **Battle of Leyte Gulf, Jap carrier *Zuiho* under attack by aircraft of USS *Enterprise*, October 25, 1944.** *Bison Picture Library*

BELOW LEFT: **The British HMS *Hermes* was the first ship to be designed from the outset as an aircraft carrier and was laid down in January 1918, although she was not completed until 1924.** *Bison Picture Library*

replace the heavy losses experienced in the Pacific fighting from 1942 onwards. Consequently, hardly any two vessels were the same and many were conversions of mercantile or naval hulls originally designed for other purposes. These included the *Hiyo* and *Junyo* (24,000 tons) which commissioned in mid-1942 and were the first Japanese carriers in which the funnel was integrated into the island superstructure, previous carriers having deck-edge funnels angled downward in an attempt to keep hot gases away from flight-deck operations. Carrying up to 53 aircraft, both were engaged in the Battle of the Philippine Sea in June 1944. *Hiyo* was sunk and *Junyo* was damaged to the extent that she was never fully operational again.

The most significant purpose-built Japanese carrier built during the war was the 29,300-ton *Taiho* which was completed in March 1944. In some respects she was very similar to the British "Illustrious" class. Capable of operating up to 75 aircraft, she also featured an armored flightdeck and this, together with extensive armor protection to the machinery spaces, accounted for approximately

Coral Sea

The Battle of the Coral Sea was the first battle to be fought entirely by carrier aircraft without the two opposing fleets coming into sight of each other. Up until May 1942 Japanese forces had progressed through the Pacific virtually without a setback and their next objective was Port Moresby in New Guinea. An American force under Rear Admiral Frank J. Fletcher, consisting of the carriers *Yorktown* and *Lexington* backed up by cruisers and destroyers, was dispatched to the Coral Sea off the coast of Australia to frustrate the invasion fleet. On the morning of May 7 aircraft from the US carriers sunk the Japanese light carrier *Shoho*, but the main battle between aircraft from both sides took place on the 8th. The Japanese carrier *Shokaku* was damaged, and in a counter-strike, the USS *Lexington* was lost. Overall, the US losses in the battle were heavier, losing a large aircraft carrier, a destroyer and a tanker, which was more than twice the total tonnage of shipping lost by the Japanese, which included a light carrier, a destroyer and several smaller vessels, although the Japanese had lost more aircraft (92) than the Americans (66), and this loss of highly trained aircrew proved difficult to replace. However, the battle was a strategic victory for the US forces. The Japanese invasion force was forced to turn back and the safety of Australia was ensured. The Japanese had lost their aura of invincibility, it being the first time in the war they had not achieved their objectives.

LEFT and BELOW LEFT: **The USS *Lexington* at the Battle of the Coral Sea. Shortly after these photos were taken the ship succumbed to previous damage from three bomb and two torpedo hits and sank after an explosion caused by leaking aviation fuel.** *Bison Picture Library*

Midway

The Battle of Midway, fought a month after the Battle of the Coral Sea, was the decisive encounter of the war in the Pacific. The Japanese, under Admiral Yamamoto, hoped to lure the American navy to an encounter in which it could be finished off by the greater numbers of capital ships in the Japanese navy. The battle, which took place on June 4-5, 1942, near the US Hawaiian island of Midway, was decided entirely by aircraft. The typically complex battle-plan of the Japanese meant that their forces became fragmented, with Admiral Nagumo's carriers becoming bunched together, detached from their support, having to both attack the American fleet and the island of Midway in preparation for invasion. The Americans, benefiting from having broken the Japanese codes, concealed their aircraft carriers, and under the command of Admiral Spruance launched two waves of air strikes. The first wave of 41 TBD Devastator torpedo-bombers was unsuccessful and 37 aircraft were lost; the second wave of 57 Dauntless dive-bombers from *Enterprise* and *Yorktown* caught the Japanese carriers with their aircraft being refueled and rearmed on deck in preparation for their second attack, and the Zero fighter cover still at low level following the encounter with the torpedo-bombers. The carriers *Akagi*, *Kaga* and *Soryu* were sunk immediately; only *Hiryu* managed to get her aircraft off, which crippled the US carrier *Yorktown* (later sunk by the Japanese submarine *I-168*), before being sunk later in the day by dive-bombers from *Enterprise*. The Japanese never recovered from the loss of their entire carrier force, over 250 aircraft and half their naval pilots.

30% of the ship's tonnage. Despite this scale of protection, her operational career was extremely short. During the Battle of the Philippine Sea she was hit by a torpedo from a US submarine on June 19, 1944, although this alone would not have caused her loss. Unfortunately, leaking aviation fuel led to a build up of petrol vapors and the ship was destroyed when these ignited a few hours later. In an attempt to rationalize carrier construction, a further six 17,000-ton carriers were laid down in 1942-43 as the "Unryu" class. They were unarmored but could operate up 65 aircraft. Only three (*Unryu*, *Amagi* and *Katsuragi*) were actually completed in late 1944, by which time a shortage of aircraft meant that they could not be employed operationally.

Japan's swansong in the carrier stakes was a real monster — the 64,800-ton *Shinano* which was originally laid down in 1940 as a "Yamato" class battleship. Early war experience demonstrated the value of aircraft carriers and a decision was made to convert the ship while still under construction on the slipway. The outcome was a ship unique not only in size but also in function, as she was not intended to operate as a conventional carrier. Instead, taking advantage of the massively armored battleship hull together with an armored flightdeck, the ship would act as a support ship for other carrier task forces. The hangar would be fitted out as an aircraft repair workshop while large quantities of fuel and ordnance could be stowed. The ship's air group was intended to comprise only some 40-50 aircraft for self-defense purposes, but up to 120 could be accommodated

LEFT: **Flightdeck of *Yorktown* after a Japanese attack.** *US Navy*

BELOW: **The Japanese carrier *Unryu* was completed in 1944 but was sunk by a US submarine within months of entering service.** *Bison Picture Library*

with the balance being held as spares and replacements for the combat carriers of a task force. The ship was heavily defended with over 150 AAA guns as well as multiple rocket launchers. In the event the concept was never put to the test as the Shinano fell prey to the US submarine *Archerfish* which put four torpedoes into her on November 29, 1944, while she was en route to Kure for final fitting out. Under normal circumstances even such major damage should not have sunk the ship, but being in a non-operational state much of her damage-control equipment and watertight doors had not been fitted.

When World War II broke out in September 1939, the aircraft carrier was an untried weapon and the battleship was still regarded as the major arbiter of seapower. Initially there was little to change this point of view. The British carrier *Courageous* was torpedoed and sunk by a U-boat within days of the outbreak of war and her sister ship *Glorious* was sunk off Norway by gunfire from the German battlecruisers *Scharnhorst* and *Gneisenau* in June 1940. However, the tables were turned in November 1940 when Swordfish torpedo bombers launched from HMS *Illustrious* attacked the Italian fleet at anchor in the harbor of Taranto

BELOW: **The British battlecruiser HMS *Repulse* escorts the liner *Queen Mary* in the early stages of the war. *Repulse* was later sunk by Japanese aircraft off Malaya in December 1941, a major setback for Britain.** *Bison Picture Library*

Taranto

The Battle of Taranto was the first time that a naval attack was carried out using carrier-based aircraft. In the first year of the war the Royal Navy's operations in the Mediterranean were seriously hampered by the numerically superior Italian navy, so a plan was devised to strike at its main base in Taranto harbor, on the south coast of Italy. On the night of November 11, 1940, Admiral Cunningham dispatched 21 Swordfish torpedo-bomber biplanes from Nos 813, 815, 819 and 824 Naval Air Squadrons. The aircraft took off from the carrier HMS *Illustrious* in two waves, and despite the anti-aircraft defenses in the harbor, inflicted severe damage on the Italian fleet with a combination of torpedo and bomb strikes, for the loss of only two aircraft. Three of the Italians' six battleships were put out of action, *Conte de Cavour*, *Duilio* and *Littorio*, and two heavy cruisers were also damaged. At a stroke the balance of naval power had shifted in the Mediterranean as the Italians moved the remainder of their fleet to ports on the western side of Italy, further away from Allied operations in the central Mediterranean. The success of this strike was to have profound repercussions in the way naval battles would be fought later in this war, not least in the Japanese attack on Pearl Harbor a year later.

on the night of November 11, 1940. Three battleships, including the modern *Littorio*, were serious damaged and put out of action for some time. Later, in May 1941, Swordfish were instrumental in slowing down the German battleship *Bismarck* in the North Atlantic so that she could be finished off by the HMS *King George V* and HMS *Nelson*. However, it was the Japanese who finally demonstrated that the ascendancy of the battleship was ending with their infamous air attack on Pearl Harbor on December 7, 1941. Five US battleships were sunk while three more were seriously damaged in a brilliantly executed attack which drew its inspiration from the earlier events at Taranto. Perhaps a more significant success for the Japanese was the sinking of the British capital ships *Prince of Wales* and *Repulse* off the Malayan coast only three days after Pearl Harbor. This was the first time the modern battleships, free to maneuver in open waters, had been sunk by air attack alone. Subsequently, most major actions involved aircraft carriers and in the closing stages of the Pacific War the mighty battleship *Yamato* met its end at the hands of US Navy aircraft in April 1945 (her sister ship, *Musashi*, was sunk by submarines).

There were relatively few occasions when battleships engaged each other in surface actions without the intervention of aircraft. One such incident ended disastrously for the Royal Navy when the battlecruiser *Hood* was destroyed by a single salvo from the *Bismarck* although the latter was

Cunningham

Admiral Sir Andrew Browne Cunningham (1883-1963), nicknamed "ABC," commanded the Fleet Air Arm's raid which inflicted serious losses on the Italian fleet at harbor in Taranto in November 1940. Although his early experience had largely been on destroyers, which he commanded in World War I, this pioneering naval attack using carrier-based aircraft led the way for many of the most significant naval battles of World War II. The next year Cunningham's fleet finally came head-to-head with the Italian fleet in a night battle off Cape Matapan, in March 1941, forcing the larger Italian fleet, which had been threatening British convoys from Egypt to Greece, to withdraw from the region after it lost five ships in the action (compared to British losses of one aircraft). His period as Commander-in-Chief of the Mediterranean Fleet of the Royal Navy (1939-41) saw this daring and aggressive leader, who none the less carefully calculated the risks of engagement based on an awareness of the Royal Navy's technological superiority, nullify the threat of the first the Italian navy and then also the German fleet in the area, helping in 1941 to keep supply lines open to besieged Malta and Tobruk, then supervising the evacuation of Allied troops from Greece and, subsequently, Crete. He later served as Eisenhower's deputy for Operation "Torch" in 1942, the Allied landings in North Africa, then supervising the naval support for the landings in Sicily and Italy in 1943. Later in 1943 he became First Sea Lord and after the war became Viscount Cunningham of Hyndhope.

Guadalcanal

The US Marines' landing on the Pacific island of Guadalcanal in the southern Solomons on August 7, 1942, countering an earlier Japanese landing, was one of the first amphibious assaults of World War II. A barrage of naval gunfire over the landing craft neutralized the Japanese defenses and the landing was largely unopposed. However, the seas around the island were the scene of a number of fierce clashes between the Japanese and US fleets for the next six months as the Japanese sought to reinforce their troops on the island. The costliest engagement started on the night of November 12-13, 1942, when the target of a Japanese force consisting of two battlecruisers (*Hiei* and *Kirishima*), three cruisers and 14 destroyers was the air-field on the US beach-head. They encountered an American force in the dark, sinking four American destroyers and two cruisers for the loss of *Hiei*. The next night the Japanese attempted another landing on the beach-head, with partial success. Again, on the night of November 14-15, Admiral Kondo attempted to bombard the beach head with the *Kirishima*, four cruisers and nine destroyers, but the force was intercepted by Rear Admiral Lee's Task Force 64, consisting of the battleships *South Dakota* and *Washington* and four destroyers. Three of the US destroyers were sunk and *South Dakota* was disabled by an electrical power failure, but *Washington*, using radar-directed fire, destroyed *Kirishima* in minutes. The fighting in and around Guadalcanal lasted for four months before the island was secured by US forces in February 1943.

subsequently sunk a few days later after a dramatic chase across the North Atlantic. The battlecruiser *Scharnhorst* was sunk by the battleship *Duke of York* in a well-fought action off North Cape on Boxing Day 1943.

In the Pacific, there were a number of battleship actions fought at night when aircraft were unable to participate. Prominent among these was the sinking of the Japanese battleship *Kirishima* by the USS *Washington* off Guadalcanal n November 1942. This success was partly due to the fact that the American battleship was equipped with radar, which helped overcome the traditional Japanese superiority in night actions. Another night action in which the Japanese were comprehensively defeated was the Battle of Surigao Strait which was one of series of actions around Leyte Gulf fought as US forces began their campaign to re-occupy the Philippines. On the night of October 25, 1944, a Japanese force including the battleships *Fuso* and *Yamashiro* attempted to transit the straits only to be met by overwhelming US surface forces, including no less than six old battleships, some survivors of Pearl Harbor, which succeeded in executing the classic naval maneuver of crossing the enemy's "T." The *Fuso* had already been sunk by destroyer torpedoes but the *Yamashiro* found herself as the main target for the US battleships whose 14-inch and 16-inch guns had the benefit of the latest fire-control radars. As the battered *Yamashiro* turned away, she was finished of with torpedoes. This fierce action was a fitting climax to centuries of naval surface warfare.

Of course the battleship found many other practical uses during the war. Their great size made them ideal flagships

ABOVE LEFT: **The battlecruiser HMS *Hood* was completed in 1920 and was the pride of the Royal Navy between the wars. She was sunk by a single salvo from the *Bismarck* in May 1941, leaving only three survivors out a crew of over 1,600.** *Bison Picture Library*

LEFT: **A German destroyer leads the *Scharnhorst*, *Gneisenau* and cruiser *Prinz Eugen* in their dramatic dash up the English Channel from Brest to their home ports in Germany— Operation "Cerebus." It was a tactical success, but a strategic failure. Their transfer meant that these ships no longer threatened the North Atlantic lifeline to Britain.** *Bison Picture Library*

RIGHT: **"Val" dive-bomber attacks *Hornet* off Guadalcanal.** *Bison Picture Library*

RIGHT: The Japanese cruiser *Takao* — this class carried 10 8-inch guns. *TRH Pictures*

Leyte Gulf

Following the US forces' landings on the Philippines on October 20, 1944, the Japanese decided to throw the remainder of their fleet into battle in a last attempt to halt the American advance. A complex plan was devised in which the carrier force under Admiral Ozawa was to lure the US Fast Carrier Force away from the transports and supporting warships in Leyte Gulf in the Philippines, which would then be destroyed by powerful Japanese surface forces led by Admiral Kurita in the center with five battleships, 12 cruisers and 15 destroyers, and Admirals Nishimura and Shima in the south with two battleships, four cruisers and eight destroyers. Although Ozawa's decoy successfully detached Halsey's main fleet to the north, Kurita's planned attack was delayed as it encountered Halsey's forces being lured away, with the loss of the battleship *Musashi*, heavy cruiser *Atago*, a cruiser and a destroyer. The light carrier USS *Princetown* was also sunk in the action, by air attack. Eventually, early on the 25th Kurita's forces entered San Bernardino Strait, heading for Leyte. There they overwhelmed an escort carrier group led by Rear Admiral Sprague, sinking three destroyers and an escort carrier before retreating in the face of air attack. The first kamikaze attacks of the war occurred later that day, sinking Sprague's carrier *St Lô*. Nishimura's branch of the southern Japanese force, meanwhile, was ambushed in Surigao Strait by a force commanded by Rear Admiral Oldendorf in the early hours of the 25th, with the loss of the battleships *Fuso* and *Yamashiro*, threee destroyers and a cruiser, only one destroyer escaping. The third action took place when Halsey's forces caught Ozawa. The carriers *Zuikaku*, *Chiyoda* and *Zuiho* were sunk by aircraft at dawn on October 25, and Halsey's ships then harried the Japanese, sinking four cruisers and four destroyers until giving up the chase the next day. Overall, in the largest naval battle ever, losses meant that Japan did not mount another serious naval operation.

as they could accommodate admirals and their staff, together with tons of communication equipment. Their massive AAA firepower made them ideal escorts for the vulnerable carriers and their great guns were used time and time again to batter shore targets during amphibious operations. But, in reality, their day was over and at the great ceremony held in Tokyo Bay on September 3, 1945, to witness the Japanese surrender, it was the massed flypast by hundreds of carrier-based aircraft which showed where the future of seapower would lie.

The various interwar naval treaties which had defined the carriers and battleships also laid down limitations for other classes of warships. In particular, the 1922 Washington treaty specified that cruisers should not exceed 10,000 tons displacement and the heaviest permitted guns were 8-inch while the later 1930 London Treaty differentiated between Type A cruisers with guns of over 6.1-inch caliber and Type B with 6.1-inch guns or lighter. These treaties resulted in a particularly interesting construction race, in which all the major powers attempted build the most powerful ships, ostensibly within the agreed limits. Probably the winners could be regarded as the German "Admiral Hipper" class and the Japanese "Takao" class. The latter mounted no less than 10 8-inch guns and the German ships only mounted eight, although this was backed up by a powerful AAA battery of 12 4.1-inch guns controlled by four high angle directors. Both classes carried torpedoes and aircraft. Subsequently, it was realized by the Allied powers that these ships were grossly in excess of the treaty limitations (c.14,000 tons), a trend followed to a lesser extent by Italy whose handsome looking "Zara" class came out at almost 12,000 tons despite reducing armor thickness in an attempt to stay within the 10,000-ton limit. Germany had laid down five "Hipper" class but only three were ever completed, although she also built five modern 6-inch gun cruisers prior to 1939, all of which featured a unique disposition of the main armament with a single triple gun turret forward and two triple mounts aft. One of these ships, *Konigsberg*, achieved the dubious distinction of becoming the first major warship to be sunk by air attack alone when she was dive-bombed by British aircraft in a Norwegian fjord in April 1940.

RIGHT: An Italian "Zara" class heavy cruiser in action, possibly at the Battle of Calabria on July 9, 1940. This was an inconclusive action between major elements of the British and Italian fleets which was terminated after the British battleship *Warspite* scored a hit on the Italian battleship *Giulio Cesare*, causing the Italian fleet to turn away behind a smoke screen. *Bison Picture Library*

Of the Axis powers, it was Japan which built cruisers in the greatest numbers as this type of warship was particularly suited to operations in the vastness of the Pacific Ocean. Initially she concentrated on a series of light scout cruiser which were little improvement on those built during World War I. A change was heralded by the small 2,900-ton *Yubari* completed in 1923 which pioneered new construction techniques to allow a relatively heavy armament (six 5.5-inch guns) on a small hull. The design principles were applied to the larger 7,000-ton "Furutaka" class of two ships which were armed with six 8-inch guns although the design work was completed prior to the signing of the Washington Treaty in 1922. Subsequently, a further pair of similar cruisers were laid down in 1924, but Japan then started building larger cruisers up to the 10,000-ton treaty limits. The resulting eight "Myoko" and "Takao" class ships presented a distinctive profile with three twin 8-inch turrets foreword and two aft, massive-looking bridge structures, and aircraft handling facilities abaft the twin funnels. By the time that these had all been launched, the 1930 London Treaty had come into force and Japan had used up her permitted quota of Type A 8-inch cruisers although she was permitted to build new Type B 6-inch armed cruisers as replacements for older and obsolete vessels. Consequently four ships of the "Mogami" class were laid down in 1931 and it was announced that they would be armed with no less than 15 6-inch guns in five triple turrets. This sent shockwaves through the world's naval community and both

Britain and the United States responded with similar designs. However the Japanese remained one step ahead as their ships were designed from the outset to have the triple 6-inch turrets replaced by twin 8-inch turrets when the opportunity arose, and this was done from 1939 onward. In fact one of the great debates in naval circles during the 1930s revolved around the varying merits of the 8-inch and 6-inch gun as main armament for cruisers. While the 8-inch fired a heavier shell over a greater distance, the 6-inch gun had a greater rate of fire and more guns could be carried on a given displacement. The effect of this was that cruiser armed with 12 6-inch guns could actually deliver a greater weight of shell, with an increased chance of a hit, over a given period than could a similar ship armed with eight 8-inch guns. This could be very telling in a night action, when ranges tended to be much shorter, at least until the advent of radar. Japan built two more 8-inch armed cruisers (*Tone* and *Chikuma*), and these were of a unique design with no less than four twin 8-inch turrets forward and a large open deck for aft for handling up to eight seaplanes. As the war progressed, the number of aircraft carried was reduced and the deck was used to mount additional light AAA guns. Both were sunk in action. Japan's subsequent

cruiser construction program was relatively insignificant with only five small 6-inch gun cruiser being completed between 1942 and 1944.

The Royal Navy, with a responsibility to protect the trade routes of the British Empire, had a standing requirement for considerable numbers of cruisers — the official requirement was for 70 such vessels. As early as 1924 the first ships of the "Kent" class were being laid down. Conforming strictly to the Washington Treaty, the ships displaced 10,000 tons and were armed with eight twin 8-inch gun mountings capable of 70° elevation. As completed they were some of the most handsome warships ever built, with triple funnels and a high freeboard giving almost a liner-like appearance. Seven "Kent" class cruiser were built, including two for the Australian navy, and these were later followed by a further six similar vessels of the "London" and "Norfolk" classes. Generically known as the "County" class, these ships gave sterling service in World War II and three were lost in action. *Dorsetshire* and *Cornwall* were sunk by Japanese air attack off Ceylon in April 1942, while HMAS *Canberra* was torpedoed by a Japanese destroyer off Savo Island on August 9, 1942. Britain also built two "York" class cruisers completed in 1930-31 and in essence

ABOVE: HMS *Suffolk*, a British "County" class cruiser, in 1941. Note the large hangar aft and the disruptive camouflage scheme. *Bison Picture Library*

LEFT: HMS *Dorsetshire* was the last of the triple-funneled "County" class cruisers to be built and was launched in 1929. She took part in the destruction of the *Bismarck* in May 1941 but was later sunk by Japanese carrier aircraft off Ceylon in April 1942. *via Leo Marriott*

these were cut down versions of the "Kent" class and were armed with only six 8-inch guns on a displacement of 8,250 tons. The second of these ships, HMS *Exeter*, was to earn undying fame in 1939 when she was fought almost to a standstill in the Battle of the River Plate which led to the eventual scuttling of the German pocket battleship Graf Spee.

However, these were to be the last 8-inch gun cruisers built for the Royal Navy, and almost all subsequent British cruiser were armed with the lighter 6-inch gun. This was originally on ground of cost, but also by the provisions of the 1930 London Naval treaty which, mainly at British instigation, effectively called a halt to the construction of 8-inch gun cruisers. Consequently a class of five "Leander" class cruisers armed with eight 6-inch guns in four twin turrets were laid down between 1930 and 1934, and these were followed by three more to a slightly modified design which were subsequently transferred to the Royal Australian Navy. These latter ships introduced the concept of arranging the boiler and engine rooms into separate independent units so that the likelihood of a total power loss as a result

143

River Plate

In many ways the Battle of the River Plate was a throw-back to the naval battles of World War I. Fought at the beginning of World War II, it was one of the last naval battles to be fought largely without radar or the threat of aerial or submarine attack. In the first months of the war the German pocket battleship *Admiral Graf Spee*, operating as a commerce raider in the South Atlantic, sank nine British merchantmen. On December 13, 1939, the *Graf Spee* was intercepted off the River Plate by a Royal Navy squadron of three cruisers, *Exeter*, *Ajax* and *Achilles*, commanded by Commodore Henry Harwood. In a series of engagements during the day, the *Exeter* was badly damaged and forced to retire, but the *Graf Spee* was forced to seek refuge in the neutral Uruguyan port of Montevideo, at the mouth of the River Plate, at the end of the day. The battle then turned into a game of bluff. The Uruguayan authorities gave the *Graf Spee* a deadline of December 17, after which the ship had to leave the port or be interned. At the same time British sources leaked spurious information that a large Royal Navy force was already in the vicinity. On December 17, the *Admiral Graf Spee's* commander, Captain Hans Langsdorff, scuttled and blew up his ship as she put to sea and committed suicide later that day.

ABOVE: **The forward 8-inch gun turrets of HMS *Exeter* showing the damage sustained at the Battle of the River Plate. By the time *Exeter* was forced to withdraw, only the after turret, firing in local control, was still in action.** *Bison Picture Library*

ABOVE LEFT: **The *Admiral Graf Spee* and her sister ships caused a sensation in naval circles when they appeared in the early 1930s. Although correctly designated *Panzerschiffe*, they were better known by the appelation "pocket battleships."** *Bison Picture Library*

LEFT: Graf Spee **in 1937.** *Bison Picture Library*

of action damage was considerably reduced. This idea had been first introduced by the US Navy in the "Omaha" class light cruisers built in the early 1920s and was subsequently applied to most major British warships. In order to further reduce cots and ensure that sufficient numbers of cruiser were available, a diminutive version of the "Leanders" armed with only six 6-inch guns was ordered in 1932. Displacing just over 5,200 tons, they were known as the "Arethusa" class and four were completed by 1937.

By the mid-1930s the need to effectively defend the fleet against air attack was well realized, and warships of all categories began to receive a significant increase in short-range automatic weapons while large vessels such as cruiser and battleships carried secondary batteries of 4.5-inch or 4-inch high angle guns. On a small cruiser such as the *Arethusa* it was difficult to fit worthwhile numbers of such guns, while still carrying a substantial main battery. Fortunately, the Royal Navy was developing a new 5.25-inch dual purpose gun which offered a high rate of fire in the AAA role, while its 80lb shell was destructive enough for most surface actions. In 1937 the first of 11 new "Dido" class light cruisers were laid down which were intended to be armed with no less than 10 5.25-inch in five twin turrets, three forward and two aft. Subsequently a further five "Modified Dido" class were ordered.

Although the "Dido" class were successful in their designed role, the trend to smaller cruiser was otherwise halted as it became apparent that Japan was building large 10,000-ton cruisers armed with 6-inch guns. In order to counter these, the Royal Navy embarked on the construction of eight 9,200-ton "Southampton" class light

cruisers armed with 12 6-inch guns in four triple mountings backed up by a secondary battery of eight 4-inch AAA guns and two of the new multiple two-pounder AAA mountings which were being widely adopted. With a pair of raked funnels and a symmetrical layout, these were handsome ships which saw some hard fighting during World War II, and three were lost to German and Italian action in the Mediterranean in 1941-42. They were followed by the two similar but larger vessels of the "Belfast" class, in which displacement rose above 10,000 tons and the AAA armament was increased. While these ships were being built, a further restriction on size arose as a result of the 1937 London Treaty in which the limit for cruisers was set at 8,000 tons. The result was the "Fiji" class of eight ships which were all under construction when war broke out and these managed to retain the same armament as the "Southampton" class on a hull some 40ft shorter. A repeat

RIGHT: **This is HMS *Newcastle* , a "Southampton" class light cruiser, painted in the standard Home Fleet dark gray at the outbreak of the war.** *Bison Picture Library*

BELOW: **Mounting 12 6-inch guns, the "Southampton" class light cruisers were laid down in response to the Japanese construction of the 10,000-ton "Mogami" class in the early 1930s.** *via Leo Marriott*

BELOW RIGHT: **The launch of HMS *Belfast* in August 1938. The turret-mounting rings can be clearly seen fore and aft, while the deck opening amidships will enable installation of the boilers and machinery to be completed.** *via Leo Marriott*

Naval Guns

The big naval gun reached its apotheosis on World War II battleships. Although international agreements in the 1920s and 1930s set the largest permissible gun at 16-inch, the largest battleships built, the Japanese *Yamoto* class, carried the most powerful guns (18.1-inch) ever taken to sea. The main batteries comprised three triple turrets, but the battleships also carried a range of smaller, automatic guns, including an arsenal of 25mm AAA guns. The 18.1-inch shells weighed 3,240lb with a maximum range of 45,000yd. The blast from these guns was so powerful that crew operations were seriously endangered when the main guns were fired. The US "South Dakota" class, by comparison, carried nine 16-inch guns (plus 29 5-inch, and up to 96 40mm, guns). The largest Royal Navy battleships, the "King George V" class, carried 10 15-inch guns, the diminished weight of the broadside theoretically compensated for by a higher rate of fire. In practice, the intricate turret safety mechanisms caused guns and turrets to frequently jam during engagements. The largest German battleship, *Tirpitz*, carried eight 15-inch guns. Ironically, these enormous capital ships became increasingly marginalized, their big guns being used mostly for off-shore barrages for invading forces. The rise of naval aviation meant that AAA guns became increasingly vital for warships, although navies were slow to install effective weaponry with the requisite high angle of fire. Consequently, even large capital ships were extremely vulnerable to aircraft attack. The Royal Navy developed dual purpose weapons, particularly the pom-pom two-pounder and 5.25-inch guns to set up AAA barrages, although these were not wholly successful. Other technological advances such as fire-control radar, optical range-finding equipment all assisted the developments in naval guns, enabling encounters to take place at longer range and at night.

ABOVE LEFT: **Gun crews stand by aboard the USS *San Juan* in 1942. This was one of class of small AAA cruisers mounting no fewer than 16 5-inch guns. The three after twin mounts are shown here, along with a quadruple 1.1-inch machine gun. The latter proved to be ineffective and was quickly replaced by more potent 20mm and 40mm guns.** *Bison Picture Library*

LEFT: **The three forward 5.25-inch gun turrets of the "Dido" class AAA cruiser HMS *Argonaut* make a striking sight as they elevate skywards.** *via Leo Marriott*

ABOVE: **Gunners on USS *Boise* (CL-47) fight off an air attack near Gela, Sicily July 10, 1943, during Operation "Husky."** *National Archives*

LEFT: **Forward triple 6-inch turrets of a US Navy "Brooklyn" class light cruiser.** *National Archives*

order for eight more similar cruisers in 1941 was never fully completed, although three ships eventually became the "Swiftsure" class of which only two saw any war service. Some of the others were completed to completely recast design some 20 years later.

With their great industrial base the American cruiser program considerably outstripped that of the Royal Navy, although it was slow to get under way between the wars. Ten 7,000-ton "Omaha" class light cruisers were completed in the early 1920s but were virtually obsolete by the start of World War II. However, the US Navy wholeheartedly embraced the concept of the 10,000-ton 8-inch gun cruiser defined by the Washington Naval Treaty and eventually built some 17 of this type between 1926, when the first of two 9,000-ton "Pensecola" class ships was laid down, and 1937, when the last of seven 10,100-ton "New Orleans" class was completed. Although the first two were armed with 10 8-inch guns in four mountings, the subsequent "Northampton," "Portland" and "New Orleans" classes carried nine 8-inch in three triple mountings. These cruisers took the brunt of the early action in the Pacific and no less than seven were lost in action. One of these was the ill-fated *Indianapolis* which was torpedoed by a Japanese submarine in July 1945 while bound from Guam to Leyte in the Pacific after having delivered the first atomic bomb to Tinian only a few days beforehand. Unfortunately, due to a breakdown in communication procedures, her loss went unrecorded for several days, and very few of her crew were subsequently rescued from the shark infested waters.

The United States was even more alarmed at reports of the large Japanese 6-inch gun cruisers and countered with the "Brooklyn" class of nine ships laid down in 1935-36. These were also armed with 15 6-inch guns and displaced just under 10,000 tons. By 1940, with the war in Europe raging and a Pacific war almost inevitable, the US Navy began construction of what can be regarded as the most successful cruiser design of all time, and certainly the one built in greatest numbers. The "Cleveland" class was based on the layout of the preceding "Brooklyns" but displacement rose to over 11,000 tons as by this time all treaty restrictions has ceased to be effective. A more balanced armament of 12 6-inch and 12 5-inch dual purpose guns was fitted, backed up by numerous light AAA guns. There was provision for up to four aircraft, although no torpedoes were carried. Altogether some 39 were ordered, to be followed by 13 improved "Fargo" class but not all of these were built, and some were converted on the stocks to aircraft carriers. The final tally was 26 "Cleveland" class and two "Fargo" class, while another "Cleveland" class ship (USS *Galveston*) was finally completed in 1958 as a guided missile-armed cruiser. Echoing British developments, America also built a number of small cruisers designed specifically for the AAA role. These were the 6,800-ton "Atlanta" class armed with up to 16 5-inch/38cal dual

ABOVE: An "Atlanta" class light cruiser engages a Japanese torpedo-bomber which can be seen passing across its bows. *Bison Picture Library*

BELOW: A partly modernized HMS *Warspite* in June 1937. Note the national colors on "B" turret, adopted during the Spanish Civil War in an attempt to prevent attacks by belligerent aircraft. *Bison Picture Library*

RIGHT: **HMS *Lookout*, one of eight "L" class destroyers completed in 1941-42. The twin 4.7-inch guns could be elevated to 50° but the mountings were heavy and consequently only one set of torpedo tubes could be shipped. Note the disruptive camouflage pattern.** *Bison Picture Library*

BELOW RIGHT: **Out of 16 "Tribal" class large destroyers built for the Royal Navy in 1937-38, only four survived the war. One of these was HMS *Nubian* shown here in 1944 having been updated by the addition of radar and a substantial light AAA battery.** *via Leo Marriott*

purpose guns and also eight 21-inch torpedo tubes. A total of 11 ships were ordered but not all were completed before 1945 and the armament disposition varied.

The design of the "Brooklyn" class formed the basis of a single 8-inch gunned cruiser, the USS *Wichita*, the last American heavy cruiser to be completed before World War II. Although the US Navy preferred this type vessel, it was prevented from building more by treaty restrictions and consequently it was not until 1941 that more were laid down. These were the "Baltimore" class and, freed from artificial restrictions, they displaced over 14,000 tons and carried an armament of nine 8-inch and 12 5-inch guns, as well as over 60 40mm and 20mm AAA weapons. They were handsome ships with a range of over 10,000 miles and were well suited to operations in the Pacific. Some 24 were ordered but only five were commissioned before the end of 1944, and several others were not completed until well after the war.

Although the capital ships of the various navies inevitably provided the core of forces engaged in most naval actions, they could not operate without the assistance and protection of the ubiquitous destroyer and these were built in their hundreds by the major powers. By the end of World War 1 Britain had produced the highly successful "V" and "W" classes and most of the destroyers built in the 1920s and 30s conformed to the same basic layout although they were larger and more heavily armed. The benchmark was set by two 1,200-ton destroyers, *Amazon* and *Ambuscade*, completed in 1926 and armed with four 4.7-inch guns and six 21-inch torpedo tubes. The basic design was refined in annual programs of eight ships plus a flotilla leader, named alphabetically in sequence from A to I. In the final "I" class, completed in 1936, displacement had risen to 1,370 tons and the number of torpedo tubes to 10 but otherwise there was little change in the intervening 10 years. When the United Sates began building destroyers again in 1932, the "Farragut" class was very similar except that the standard weapon was the 5-inch/38cal. The ensuing "Mahan," "Gridley" and "Benham" classes were similar while by the outbreak of war, the slightly larger Benson/ Livermore and Bristol classes were under construction and

in these displacement had risen to 1,650 tons and an extra 5-inch gun was shipped. By 1941 production had standardised on the 2,000-ton flush-decked "Fletcher" class which carried a much heavier light AAA armament. It is sobering to look at the statistics of American production, which almost outstripped the rest of the world's navies combined. From the outbreak of war she produced no fewer than 417 fleet destroyers including no less than 175 "Fletcher" class and 72 of the preceding "Bristol" class.

Apart from these relatively conventional destroyers, the US Navy was drawn into a trend to build larger and more powerfully armed destroyers which had been started by the Japanese with the "Fubuki" class first laid down in 1926. Displacing some 1,750 tons, they were armed with six 5-inch guns in twin mountings and carried nine torpedo tubes. More significant, but unknown by the allies at the time, the torpedoes were the notorious 24-inch Long Lance weapons which were faster, longer-ranged and carried a heavier

LEFT: **HMS *Gallant*, a typical British destroyer of the 1930s. She is armed with four 4.7-inch guns and carries eight 21-inch torpedo tubes.** *via Leo Marriott*

BELOW: **The ultimate British wartime destroyer was the "Battle" class, which featured a powerful radar-directed AAA armament. The first units were rushed to the Pacific to assist in defending the British Pacific Fleet against Japanese kamikaze attacks but arrived too late to see any action.** *via Leo Marriott*

BOTTOM: **The "L" and "M" class, completed in 1941-42, were perhaps the most handsome destroyers ever built for the Royal Navy. They were also the first to have their main armament in fully enclosed gun turrets, in this case three twin 4.7-inch mountings.** *via Leo Marriott*

warhead than the standard British and American 21-inch torpedoes. All subsequent Japanese destroyers were similar to the "Fubukis" and there ultimate development was the 2,500 ton *Shimikaze* which was capable of almost 40 knots. Another technically advanced Japanese design was the "Akitsuki" class of AAA escort destroyers built during the war which were armed with eight semi-automatic 3.9-inch long-barreled AAA guns.

The original "Fubuki" class had prompted other countries to build similar vessels including the Italian "Soldato" class (1,900 tons, six 4.7-inch guns, six torpedoes tubes), the British "Tribal" class (1960 tons, eight 4.7in guns, four 21-inch torpedo tubes) and the US "Porter" (1,850 tons, eight 5-inch guns, eight 21-inch torpedoes tubes) and "Somers" (1,850 tons, eight 5-inch guns and 12 21-inch torpedoes tubes). However, the ultimate developer of the so called super-destroyer was France which embraced the

concept with great enthusiasm, building several variants culminating in the 3,000-ton "Mogador" class of which two were completed in 1938. Armed with eight 5.5-inch guns and 10 torpedo tubes, these strikingly handsome vessels could make 39 knots in war trim and were credited with 43 knots in trial conditions. These particular ships were scuttled at Toulon in November 1942, but some of the preceding "Le Fantasque" class had a very eventful war

before being refitted in America and fought actively with the allies in the Mediterranean.

With a relatively short construction time, most countries were able to build new destroyers which incorporated the hard learnt lessons from some of the early engagements. The principle trend was to increase AAA firepower with Britain in particular having lost substantial numbers of destroyers to air attack during in the first half of the war. Unfortunately it was not until the "Battle" class entered service in late 1944 that the Royal Navy finally deployed a destroyer with a effective dual purpose main armament consisting of high angle 4.5-inch guns in power-operated turrets, although in the meantime significant numbers of 1,500 ton Emergency Program destroyers were built. On the other hand, the US Navy had available the excellent 5-inch/38 cal dual purpose gun which armed all of its destroyers throughout the war. By the end of 1943 the "Sumner" class destroyer armed with six 5-inch in three twin turrets was entering service and this were subsequently followed by the similar but slightly larger "Gearing" class. Again, these were produced in large numbers, a total of 170 ships of both classes being eventually produced, although many of the "Gearings" were completed postwar.

German destroyer development to some extent followed the French example, in that their later ships were armed with heavy caliber 5.9-inch guns. The original "von Roeder" and "Maas" classes built prior to 1939 were fairly

LEFT: **The "Buckley" class destroyer escort was originally designed to Royal Navy specifications, but it was adopted on a grand scale by the US Navy. The most famous of these was the USS *England*, shown here, which achieved the unequaled feat of sinking no less than six Japanese submarines within the space of 12 days in May 1944. Unfortunately, this gallant ship was seriously damaged by air attack off Okinawa on May 9, 1945, and was subsequently scrapped.**
Bison Picture Library

BELOW LEFT: **A US "Livermore" class destroyer lays a smoke screen during the landings at Salerno, Italy, in September 1943. Note the recognition silhouettes of enemy Italian aircraft on the spray dodger of the ship in the foreground.** *Bison Picture Library*

BELOW: **The crew of HMS *Prince of Wales* abandons ship as the battleship lists to port after being hit by Japanese torpedoes. The battlecruiser HMS *Repulse* was also sunk in this same engagement.** *Bison Picture Library*

ABOVE: **An early American gesture in support of Britain was the provision of 50 old US Navy World War I destroyers in 1940. Shown here is HMS *Clare* (ex-USS *Abel P. Upshur*) which has had two boilers and funnels removed to allow the installation of long-range fuel tanks. A new utilitarian bridge has also been fitted.** *Bison Picture Library*

ABOVE LEFT: **A Royal Navy "Tribal" class destroyer in the Mediterranean. One of the after twin 4.7-inch gun mountings has been replaced a twin 4-inch high-angle mounting in an attempt to boost the ship's anti-aircraft firepower, a critical deficiency in most British destroyers throughout the war.** *Bison Picture Library*

LEFT: **A stirring postwar view of HMS *Charity*, one of the last group of the wartime Emergency Program destroyers to be completed. She was sold to Pakistan in 1958 and scrapped in 1982.** *Bison Picture Library*

conventional with an armament of five single 5-inch guns and eight torpedo tubes, although at around 2,200 tons displacement they were considerably large than contemporary British destroyers. Despite this advantage, many were sunk in the fierce Battle of Narvik in April 1940. Their subsequent replacements were larger and originally mounted four single 5.9-inch guns although from 1942 onwards most were modified to carry a total a five guns with a twin turret foreword and three single mounts aft. In all Germany only managed to build a total of 39 modern large destroyers up to 1944, and completion of further vessels was prevented by allied bombing. However the Kriegsmarine also deployed up to 50 torpedo boats of displacement varying between 900 and 1,300 tons and some of these were effectively destroyers. The "T22" ("Elbing") class, for example, mounted four 4.1-inch guns, a dozen light AAA guns and six 21-inch torpedo tubes and could make 33 knots.

Although the German surface fleet included powerful and modern warships, it was completely outranked in size

by the British and American navies and, as the war progressed, it was under increasingly heavy air attack. The most dangerous threat to the allied cause came from Germany's ever expanding U-boat fleet. As submarine construction was not officially permitted until 1935, by the time war broke out in 1939 their were only 57 U-boats in commission, and many of these were undergoing refits or were only suitable for training duties. Nevertheless they quickly made their presence felt and sank the British aircraft carrier HMS *Courageous* on September 17, 1939, and the battleship *Royal Oak* at Scapa Flow on October 14. Other capital ships were seriously damaged by mines laid by U-boats and by the end of the year many merchant ships had also been sunk. By June 1940 Germany had occupied Norway and France and the U-boats were now able to use forward bases to deploy in ever increasing numbers against the convoys carrying food and vital war supplies to the British Isles. The grim and relentless Battle of the Atlantic began in earnest, and by 1945 when the war ended, some 21 million tons of allied shipping had been sunk at the cost of 785 U-boats destroyed. It was a battle in which technology and science played a vital role, as both sides sought to keep one step ahead of the other. Initially the U-boats had a relatively easy time as, although an effective convoy system was established as soon as war broke out, there were just not enough suitable escorts vessels available to protect them. In addition, the Royal Navy had been somewhat complacent before the war as it considered that its Asdic systems, developed in World War I, were capable of detecting and tracking submarines with enough accuracy to allow effective attacks with depth charges. Sadly this proved not to be the case, and in any event the German tactics of attacking on the surface at night with groups of U-boats (wolfpacks) rendered Asdic (or Sonar as it was later known) virtually useless.

The eventual defeat of the U-boats had to await the widespread adoption of radar aboard escort vessels, the development of new anti-submarine weapons such as

Mine Warfare

First seriously used in the Russo-Japanese war 1904-05, underwater mines were an extremely effective and cheap anti-shipping and anti-submarine weapon during World War II, used particularly to defend harbors, straits or potential invasion sites, although they were also laid to disrupt enemy shipping off hostile coastlines. The mines were anchored in position by a length of cable and activated when the vessel came into contact with or close proximity to the mine. Many variations in mines were used including influence mines, those with pressure fuses, acoustic pistols, delayed-action mines and magnetic mines that could be set to be activated by the specific magnetic field of an enemy vessel. Mines were laid by a variety of vessels including submarines, as well as aircraft. Specialized mine-clearing vessels were used to combat the threat of mines. At the Normandy landings, mine countermeasures (MCM) vessels followed by dan-laying trawlers marking the channels with small marker buoys ("dans") were used to clear and keep open channels through each mine barrier. Nevertheless, about half the Allied ships lost at Normandy were sunk by mines. Many mines were also fitted with explosive anti-sweeping devices which broke the clearing wires of minesweepers. The Allies also used Royal Navy frogmen or US Navy/Marine Corps Underwater Demolition teams to clear mine-defended beaches prior to amphibious assault.

ABOVE LEFT: **The 750-ton Type VII U-boat was the mainstay of Germany's submarine force in the early part of the war. This is *U-52*, a Type VIIB, and unlike virtually all of her sister boats she survived the war but was scuttled at Kiel in May 1945.** *Bison Picture Library*

LEFT: **The introduction of very long-range escort aircraft from early 1943 onward was instrumental in the defeat of the U-boat. This shot shows *U-848*, a Type IXD, actually under attack from a US Navy PB4Y Privateer (Navy version of Liberator bomber). Assisted by a USAAF B-25 Mitchell, the attack was ultimately successful and *U-848* was sunk some 290 miles southwest of Ascension Island.** *Bison Picture Library*

Hedgehog and Squid, and the provision of air support across the whole of the North Atlantic. In the early war years the escorts for the convoys were made up from a mixed bag of warships including converted destroyers and small corvettes. These latter were based on a commercial whale catcher design and were originally intended for coastal escort duties. However, several hundred were eventually built as the "Flower" class and they performed sterling service in the North Atlantic despite gaining a well-deserved reputation for being overcrowded and uncomfortable. However, experience led to the concept of

FAR RIGHT: **The "Flower" class corvette was adapted from a commercial whaler design in 1939, and just under 300 were produced in Britain, Canada and the United States. They formed the backbone of the allied convoy escort forces until larger and better equipped escorts became available from 1943 onwards. Shown here is one of the first to be completed, HMS *Azalea*.** *Bison Picture Library*

RIGHT: **Friedrich Eckoldt, a German "Maas" class destroyer, seen during the occupation of Norway in April 1940. Several of her sister ships were sunk by British forces in the battle of Narvik but although she avoided a similar fate, she was eventually sunk by the cruisers HMS *Sheffield* and HMS *Jamaica* in December 1942.** *Bison Picture Library*

Battle of the Atlantic

One of the most significant battles of World War II, the Battle of the Atlantic was fought for the duration of the war for control of the vital transatlantic trade routes, largely between German U-boats and Allied merchant shipping supported by warship escorts. The battle reached its peak in the spring of 1943 when Dönitz's tactic of concentrating U-boats in attacks on convoys in "wolfpacks," beyond the reach of shore-based supporting aircraft, was causing huge losses of Allied shipping and personnel and seriously threatening Britain's ability to continue the war. The tide was turned by a combination of factors, perhaps most significantly the Allies growing understanding of the potential of air power at sea. Convoy tactics became increasingly effective, especially through the use of carrier escorts and long-range aircraft, backed up by the new technologies of radar and sonar and the breaking of the German "Enigma" naval codes. By the end of the war the prodigious output from US shipyards had made good Allied losses but the German losses had become unsustainable – 753 U-boats sunk out of an operational total of 863, and over 28,000 men losing their lives — and after the great convoy battles of spring 1943 the U-boats were in retreat from the North Atlantic.

a larger, purpose-designed, anti-submarine vessel which was originally known as a twin-screw corvette. Named after British rivers, the new ships began to enter service in 1943 and were subsequently known as frigates, reviving this title for the first time since the sailing navy had faded away in the 19th century.

Crunch time in the North Atlantic was the spring of 1943 when the sinking of allied merchant ships was substantially reduced while, at the same time, so many U-Boats were lost that the German High Command temporarily ordered their withdrawal. Thereafter, although the U-boat menace remained, it was kept in check until the end of the war. Despite this, Germany introduced several major technical developments including the use of the schnorkel mast (actually a Dutch invention) which enabled a submarine to run its diesel engines while cruising at periscope depth. However, its greatest advance was the Type XXI U-boat which radically altered thinking on underwater operations. Previously a submarine's speed while submerged and powered by batteries was relatively slow, typically around six knots, and the surface speed on diesels was usually two or three times greater. In the Type XXI, the whole vessel was optimized for its underwater task. Battery capacity was substantially increased, and these could be kept constantly charged by the diesel engines while the boat ran with its schnorkel raised. The hull and conning tower were completely streamlined, and the combination of this and the increased battery power meant that the Type XXI could manage up to 16 knots for short periods underwater, as fast

ABOVE: **A Hedgehog anti-submarine mortar on the foredeck of a British escort. This type of weapon conferred a great tactical advantage over the conventional depth charge as it could be fired ahead of the ship while sonar contact was still held, greatly increasing the chance of a kill.** *Bison Picture Library*

as some of the surface escorts. Coupled with improved sonar systems and guided torpedoes, the Type XXI was a formidable weapon system which, fortunately for the Allies, could not be built in sufficient numbers to have a major effect before the end of the war. However it was to have a major influence on postwar submarine design. Germany was also developing other designs such as the Type XVII and XXVIII, which were powered by Walter closed-cycle turbines that required no external air supply. These were capable of sustained high underwater speeds and would have posed serious problems if they had been fully operational before 1945.

Although the German U-boats formed the largest submarine fleet during World War II, it is often forgotten that American submarines had major successes in the Pacific and sank almost 1,000 Japanese merchantmen as well as a third of all the Japanese warships lost in action. American submarines were much larger than most contemporary British and German craft, as they were designed for long patrols in the Pacific and consequently had increased bunkerage, additional torpedoes and larger crew accommodation areas. The standard wartime production design was

Dönitz

Grand Admiral Karl Dönitz (1891-1980) is most associated with the U-boat arm of the German navy. He served on U-boats in World War I from 1916 until he was captured by the British when his command *UB-69* was sunk in 1918. In the interwar years he was a fervent advocate of the potential of U-boats in naval warfare and became a Nazi Party supporter so by the time Germany was preparing a new U-boat fleet for war in 1939 Dönitz had been placed in charge of its operations and strategy. His success in developing the "wolfpack" strategy of mass attacks on all Allied shipping led to his eventually succeeding Raeder as Supreme Commander of the Kriegsmarine in 1943. The Battle of the Atlantic seriously threatened Allied supply lines for a while but the increasingly high losses in the U-boat fleet led Dönitz to gradually withdraw the fleet from the front line in the North Atlantic. Hitler nominated Dönitz as his successor and he became the head of state after Hitler's death in April 1945 until the final surrender to the Allies the next month. He was tried at Nuremberg in 1946 and sentenced to 10 years' imprisonment for war crimes.

the "Gato" class which began entering service at the end of 1941 and, together with the subsequently similar "Balao" and "Tench" classes, was built in great numbers. This displaced 1,500 tons in surface trim and carried a total of 24 21-inch torpedoes fired from six bow and four stern tubes. They could make 20 knots on the surface and were often deployed in wolfpacks in the same manner as the German U-boats.

Although Britain had also built some large 1,500-ton boats in the decade following World War I, in the early 1930s this trend was reversed with appearance of the highly successful "S" class which displaced around 670 tons on the surface. These boats were well-suited to operations in the North Sea and Mediterranean, and consequently they remained in production right up to the end of the war with over 60 being commissioned. The even smaller (540 tons) "U" and "V" classes, originally conceived as training submarines, were also built in some numbers but they had a severely restricted operational radius. As war approached, production of the 1,100-ton "T" class began, and these were heavily armed with 10 torpedo tubes. When the Royal Navy began to build up operations in the Far East, they were the only British submarines with the range for operations in Southeast Asia from bases in Australia. However, they still did not compare favorably with their American contemporaries and they could only stay on their patrol station for short periods.

A feature of submarine construction between the wars was an attempt by many navies to produce a large submarine cruiser, the basic idea being that it could surface and sink ships with gunfire rather than with expensive torpedoes. Britain built a prototype *X-1* which could make 20 knots on the surface and was armed with four 5.2-inch guns in twin turrets while the US Navy completed three "Argonaut"/ "Narwhal" class armed with two 6-inch guns. Neither navy persisted with this type of vessel and the X-1 was decommissioned before 1939. The most interesting design was the French *Surcouf* which displaced 4,200 tons (submerged) and was armed with twin 8-inch guns as well as carrying a small seaplane in a hangar aft of the conning tower. Completed in 1934, she had a chequered wartime career after escaping to Britain in 1940 but was sunk in collision with a US merchant ship in February 1942.

The one navy to persist with the cruiser submarine was Japan, which built them in large numbers, typical design being the "I15" class of which 20 were completed. These displaced 2,500 tons on the surface and were armed with a single 5.5-inch guns, six 21-inch torpedo tubes and carried an aircraft. The ultimate Japanese development was the "I400" class of which a few were completed before the end of the war. These 3,500-ton monsters carried no less than three seaplanes. Japan also built substantial numbers of more conventional patrol submarines as well as various midget submarines, some intended as underwater suicide

Normandy

The naval back-up to the Normandy landings by the Allies was vital. Operation "Neptune" was to be the largest amphibious operation in the war in Europe, being supported by seven battleships, 23 cruisers, over 100 destroyers — over 700 warships in total under the overall command of Admiral Ramsey, plus about 7,000 landing vessels. Allied air superiority ensured that the naval operation proceeded largely undisturbed. Following a massive naval bombardment of the German's "Atlantic Wall" shore defenses, 155,000 American, Canadian and British troops were landed on five beaches — "Omaha" and "Utah" (US), "Gold" and "Sword" (British) and "Juno" (Canadian) — by a fleet of over 5,000 vessels. The troops and equipment were landed in a variety of specialized landing craft: often transferring from the larger ocean-going transports, attack cargo ships, dock landing ships and tank landing ships into small utility landing craft. These craft could be beached and their bow doors opened and/or a ramp lowered. They were also supported by a variety of specialized landing craft armed with guns, mortars and rockets. Over the next three days, as the beachheads were established, the fleet suffered minimal losses, Kriegsmarine torpedo boats accounting for the Norwegian destroyer *Svenner*, the Royal Navy frigate HMS *Lawford* being lost to air attack, and HMS *Wrestler*, USS *Corry,* the US minesweeper *Tide*, the US destroyers *Meredith* and *Glennon,* and the destroyer escort *Rich* being sunk by mines. On June 9 over 50 old merchant ships and warships were scuttled off the beaches to create the artificial "Mulberry" harbors to help supply the Allied forces.

ABOVE: **The Landing Ship Tank was one of many specialist vessels built to facilitate amphibious operations. Their shallow draft and bow doors enabled heavy armored vehicles to transported directly onto beachheads.**
Bison Picture Library

ABOVE LEFT: **The Mulberry artificial harbor established off the Normandy coast following the successful D-Day landings. Construction of this facility enabled deep-draft supply ships to offload directly to the shore and was essential in maintaining the build up of the allied armies after the initial assault.** *Bison Picture Library*

LEFT: **A variety of landing craft shown during the Normandy landings, June 1944. In the foreground are two LCVPs (Landing Craft Vehicle and Personnel) used to transfer troops from ships anchored offshore to the beach. Behind them on the left is a 250-ton LCI(L) — Landing Craft Infantry (Large) from which troops could disembark by means of ramps lowered either side of the bow.**
Bison Picture Library

RIGHT: **Man the boats! US Marines climb down scrambling nets to board waiting LCVPs ready to move ashore. The ship is the Attack Transport USS** *McCawley* **which was torpedoed and sunk on June 30, 1943, during an operation to take New Georgia in the Central Solomons.** *Bison Picture Library*

LEFT: **D-Day — British troops prepare to move inland from "Gold" beach as a steady shuttle of landing craft bring reinforcements while others are stranded on the beach by the falling tide.** *Bison Picture Library*

craft. These could also be carried by the larger submarines instead of the normal seaplanes. Overall, Japanese submarines did not achieve the success which might have been expected given the numbers deployed. This was partly due to the efficient anti-submarine technology of the US Navy but also due to the fact that Japan's tactical doctrine was to employ submarines in conjunction with their surface fleet and such operations rarely worked out as planned.

One aspect of the naval warfare which matured considerably during World War II was the concept of amphibious warfare, in particular the landing of substantial forces against heavily defended coastlines. In World War I there were few such operations, and in all cases landings were made using standard ships boats and towed barges and lighters. By 1939 as the requirement for more specialized craft was realized, very few had actually been built. The first major operation of World War II was the invasion of French Northwest Africa in November 1942. This was followed in by Operation "Husky" to occupy Sicily in July 1943, and landings at Anzio and Salerno on the Italian mainland in late 1943 and early 1944. However these were all eclipsed by the massive Operation "Overlord" in June 1944 when Allied troops landed in force over the Normandy beaches in Northwest France.

These great setpiece operations were mirrored in the Pacific where US forces spent three years following a twin-pronged attack on the Japanese homeland. From the southeast US forces gradually fought their way from Guadalcanal (the cause of several major naval battles), and New Guinea, through to the Philippines. From the east, Admiral Nimitz masterminded the inspired island-hopping campaign which ranged through the Central Pacific to terminate in the bloody battles for Okinawa and Iwo Jima. To sustain these operations, a massive range of new and specialized ships came into service. The main types were the various landing craft and landing ships to ferry troops and armored vehicles directly to the beaches. These were supported by large transports and major vessels such as the LSD (Landing Ship Dock) which could carry several landing craft in a floodable stern well. In addition many landing craft were modified to provide close-in fire support with a variety of weapons including guns, rocket projectors and

Okinawa/Iwo Jima

As US forces leap-frogged islands in the Pacific, approaching Japan, the fighting became ever more intense. The amphibious landings on the islands of Iwo Jima and Okinawa in 1945 to gain valuable airfields and anchorages, were very hard-fought. Iwo Jima was the largest all-Marine amphibious operation of the war, and although the Japanese shore defenses were pounded in a massive air and naval bombardment prior to the 4th and 5th Division Marines' invasion in February 1945, in the five-week battle to take the island the 21,000-strong Japanese garrison fought to the death, the US Marine Corps suffering 23,000 casualties. Okinawa was the last US amphibious assault before the planned invasion of Japan. Again a massive air and naval bombardment preceded the assault, the US Marines and Army meeting little resistance on their landing in April 1945. Again, the fighting to take the island was severe, and the US troops took three months to secure the island. US Navy losses were also high. Although the Japanese fleet had been neutralized by this date and its air power weakened, the US Fifth Fleet, which supported the landings, suffered the highest US Navy casualties of the war, many from kamikaze suicide attacks by the Japanese. US Navy personnel killed or wounded totaled 9,831, with 22 of the fleet's 525-strong complement of fighting ships sunk and a further 254 damaged, and 14 landing craft sunk and a further 117 damaged.

RIGHT: **A close call for USS *Missouri* at Okinawa as a Japanese fighter attempts a kamikaze attack.** *Bison Picture Library*

Halsey and Spruance

Admiral Raymond Spruance (1886-1969) and Vice Admiral William "Bull" Halsey (1882-1959) were the two leading US naval commanders in the war in the Pacific. Although temperamentally different — Spruance having a reputation for caution and Halsey being more headstrong — both played vital roles in reversing the Japanese forces' initial rapid advance in the Pacific. Spruance rose to prominence when he successfully assumed command at the Battle of Midway in 1942 after Admiral Fletcher's carrier had been earlier put out of action at the Battle of the Coral Sea, and later that year Halsey was involved in the first US counter-invasion at Guadalcanal. Under Admiral Nimitz, both Spruance's 5th Fleet and Halsey's 3rd Fleet leap-frogged the most heavily-defended enemy islands to keep the US momentum going in the campaigns in the Solomon Islands and the Gilbert and Marshall Islands. They pioneered new naval strategies using carrier forces, with their air power, and amphibious landings, which helped turn the tide in the war in the favor of the Americans. Spruance was later overall commander at the Battle of the Philippine Sea in 1944, where he received some criticism for his defensiveness in delaying the use of aircraft, and Halsey's last major conflict at the Battle of Leyte Gulf later that year was also controversial, where some felt he left the fleet dangerously exposed when he split his forces to follow a Japanese feint. Spruance later commanded naval forces at the amphibious landings on Okinawa and Iwo Jima in 1945.

mortars. Several old destroyers were converted to act as high-speed transports. In order to co-ordinate the activities of these large armadas, specialist headquarters ships were introduced. Initially these were often conversions of existing merchant ships, but several purpose-designed "Amphibious Force Flagships" were also built.

Many of the advances in the fighting efficiency of warships related to the development of electronic equipment such as radar and sonar. Although most navies had some form of rudimentary radar for range-finding purposes available at the outbreak of war, the allied forces gained a commanding lead in this field, and by 1945 all warships sprouted a conspicuous range of aerials and antenna related to a variety of specialized radar systems. Apart from the detection of surface and aerial targets, radars were also used for gunnery control and target-tracking. As the speed of attacking aircraft increased, radar-directed gunfire was essential, all the more so as the Germans introduced the first successful anti-ship missiles in 1943 and Japanese resorted to kamikaze suicide attacks in 1944. However, radars could be monitored and jammed, as could the guidance signals to airborne missiles, and these weaknesses were exploited by both sides as the concept of electronic warfare was born and had reached a surprising state of maturity by 1945. The conduct of carrier task forces introduced the need for effective control of the naval air war and radar-assisted fighter-direction tactics pioneered by the British in 1940 led to sophisticated combat information centers (CIC) aboard major warships. In the undersea war a range of sonars was developed which could detect and track submarines as well as providing the accurate range and bearing information required to prosecute a successful attack. Many of these technical innovations which had their roots in World War II formed the basis of the systems found in today's modern warships and whose development is covered in the next chapter.

LEFT: **Halsey.** *Bison Picture Library*

RIGHT: **Spruance, Nimitz, Forest Sherman (back to camera) aboard USS *New Jersey*, August 4, 1944.** *National Archives*

Radar and Sonar

Radar (radio detection and ranging) and sonar (sound navigation and ranging), although developed during the 1930s, were relatively untried at the outbreak of the war, but by 1945 their value in the war at sea was undeniable. Working separately, Britain, Germany, France and the US developed radar to allow targets to be detected beyond human visibility, and guns to be controlled at hitherto impossible ranges and in all weather conditions, day or night. The advantage bestowed by radar was dramatically underlined when the Royal Navy won a notable victory against the radar-less Italian Navy in the dark at the Battle of Cape Matapan in 1941. The Allies' new 10cm radar equipment, which replaced the original 1.7m frequency and was fitted to aircraft and warships, proved much more successful in tracking U-boats, partly because the U-boat search receivers were unable to detect the new short-wave transmissions. Sonar (known by the British during the war as "Asdic"), in spite of its limitations — it was unable to give a depth reading (although the later Type 147 could give an estimation), fixed in direction and interrupted during attack — allowed the Allies to pinpoint U-boats underwater either passively, listening for sounds made by the target, or actively, by transmitting an acoustic pulse which would be reflected off the target. Together, these advances in electronic warfare were vital in the Battle of the Atlantic.

ABOVE LEFT: **A view of HMS** *Sheffield* **(a "Southampton" class cruiser) taken just after World War II. Particularly noticeable in this shot are the many radar and communication aerials which festoon the ship, an indication of the technological advances made during the war.** *Bison Picture Library*

LEFT: **The "Black Swan" class sloops were the best British escorts deployed during the Battle of the Atlantic but they were too complex for large scale production. This is HMS** *Starling* **which was the lead ship of the escort group commanded by the ace U-boat killer, Captain F. J. Walker.**
Bison Picture Library

Today and Tomorrow
NUCLEAR POWER & GUIDED MISSILES

The surrender of Japan on September 3, 1945, brought to an end the greatest naval war ever fought and, almost overnight, made redundant the great fleets assembled by the allied powers. One immediate result was the cancellation many existing contracts to build new warships, a process which had begun early in 1945 when ultimate victory seemed assured, and this resulted in many partially completed vessels being broken up on the slipways, while others were launched and then laid up without being completed. They joined many older vessels which, worn out with war service, had already been laid up awaiting the final voyage to the breakers' yards. In addition, in the months and years following the end of hostilities, many ships from the active fleets were withdrawn from service and laid up in reserve from whence they could be rapidly recommissioned should the need arise. In such circumstances, the Allied navies were generally able to retain only the most modern ships for active duty.

Experience during the war had clearly shown that the aircraft carrier was now the arbiter of seapower, and that the day of the battleship was over. Although they could still carry out some important secondary tasks, the battleship's great drain on manpower meant that their retention in the modern postwar fleet could not be justified. Despite this, Britain persevered with the completion of her last battleship, HMS *Vanguard*, which commissioned in 1946 and the French also completed the *Jean Bart* which had been laid up incomplete for most of the war. The US Navy quickly scrapped the older battleships but retained most of the wartime construction for a little longer, while the four 45,000-ton "Iowa" class actually had quite an active postwar career almost up to the present day although they are

Tonkin Bay Yacht Club

The American involvement in the Vietnam War (1964-75) was based at sea as well as on land. Over the course of the war the "Tonkin Bay Yacht Club" became the American nickname for US Navy operations off the coast of Vietnam. One of the earliest incidents took place off the Tonkin Gulf in on August 2, 1964, when three North Vietnamese ex-Soviet "P-4" class torpedo boats attacked the US destroyer *Maddox*, claiming it was violating North Vietnamese waters, then two days later attacking the *Maddox* again and the *Turner Joy*. The US Navy, which had been supporting a South Vietnamese attack on Communist-held islands, retaliated with massive carrier air strikes, sinking 25 North Vietnamese naval vessels and destroying fuel bases. Throughout the war the US Navy allowed suppplies to be maintained, carried out coastal bombardments and used carriers as a base for inland aircraft attack. Many operations were carried out along the waterways of the Mekong Delta using US Navy SEALs (Sea, Air and Land teams), special forces first introduced in the Vietnam War, frequently backed up navy helicopters and, after 1967, the joint US Navy and US Army Mobile Riverine Force (MRF). As in the attack on the Viet-Cong at Can Giouc, June 19, 1967, assault boats supported by helicopter gunships led the attack from the Mobile Riverine Force Base, with support from naval gunfire, artillery and air strikes.

FAR LEFT: **The US Navy retained the four "Iowa" class battleships almost into the 21st century. This shot of USS *Wisconsin* was taken during the 1991 Gulf War and, while still retaining her mighty 16-inch guns, she also carries four Phalanx CIWS for self-defense against air and missile attack and deploys armored launch cells for the Tomahawk land attack cruise missile.** *Bison Picture Library*

LEFT: **Britain's last battleship was HMS *Vanguard* which was not completed until 1946 and was subsequently scrapped in 1960 despite plans at one stage to convert her to a guided-missile ship.** *via L.Marriott*

ABOVE: **An awe-inspiring demonstration of firepower by the 16-inch guns of the battleship USS *Iowa* in 1984. The effectiveness of the heavy guns in supporting amphibious operations was one of the reasons why these ships were retained for so long.**
Chrysalis Images

RIGHT: **HMS *Ark Royal* was Britain's last conventional fleet carrier. Although laid down in 1943, she was not finally commissioned until 1955. She subsequently underwent several major refits and in her final configuration, shown here, she was capable of operating Phantom jet fighters and Buccaneer nuclear strike aircraft. She was retired in 1978 and scrapped shortly thereafter.**
via L.Marriott

Gulf War

The coalition of forces which came together to counter Iraq's attack on Kuwait in August 1990 fought as a United Nations force. To complement the massive airlift, in the build-up of Operation "Desert Shield," much of the heavy armor was transported by sea, some in chartered merchant vessels, some in specialist landing ships. By the time the build-up of forces was complete, at the end of the year, the naval blockade in the Gulf comprised the small navies of the Gulf States, plus warships from the USA, UK, Russia, Denmark, Canada and Norway. In the Arabian Sea and Red Sea further coalition warships came from France, Argentina, Australia, Italy, the Netherlands, Spain, Belgium and Greece. In the ensuing conflict, the Iraqi navy was neutralized by the large coalition surface fleet, 23 Iraqi warships and 18 auxiliary vessels being sunk by coalition aircraft. The main threat to the coalition fleet was mines, as the Iraqi Exocet-armed missiles and aircraft were all knocked out and the single threatening "Silkworm" anti-ship missile was shot down by a Sea Dart anti-aircraft missile. In the main land attack on Iraq, Operation "Desert Storm," US Navy ships were used to fire a large number of General Dynamics Tomahawk cruise missiles against heavily defended targets in Iraq, as well as the shorter-range Stand-off Land Attack Missiles (SLAMs), in preparation for the rapid defeat of the Iraqi forces.

now permanently decommissioned. After seeing action in the Korean War in the early 1950s, they were brought out of reserve to provide fire support for operations in Vietnam. Then, in the 1980s, they were modernized and equipped to fire the Tomahawk long-range cruise missiles, which were most effectively deployed in the 1991 Gulf War.

While the battleship was fading from the naval scene, the focus of seapower was now centered on the aircraft carrier. By 1945 the US Navy, in particular, had reached a peak of efficiency and deployed substantial numbers of the large "Essex" class carriers, while the three new "Midway" class were just entering service. The British were not so well off. Although their fleet carriers of the "Illustrious" and "Implacable" classes had fought a hard war, they were of limited usefulness in the postwar era as their armored decks led to restricted headroom in the hangars so that there was difficulty in accommodating the new generations of larger naval aircraft. This problem was not solved until the new 40,000-ton carriers *Eagle* and *Ark Royal* commissioned in the early 1950s, having been first laid down during the war. Fortunately for the Royal Navy, towards the end of the war they had developed the "Colossus" and "Majestic" class

light fleet carriers which were constructed to mercantile standards to speed construction and reduce costs, and were powered by standard destroyer machinery. Although smaller than the fleet carriers, they proved capable of operating most aircraft and were much more economic to run in terms of both cost and manpower. They provided the backbone of British carrier operations in the early postwar years and served with distinction in the Korean War. Others, not required by the Royal Navy, were sold to various Commonwealth and other navies including Canada, Australia, India, France and the Netherlands. Some eventually found their way to South America and at least one, the Brazilian *Mineas Gerias* (ex-HMS *Vengeance* launched in 1944), is still available for service today.

In the closing stages of World War II several land-based air forces had begun to operate jet combat aircraft and it was only a matter of time before they went to sea. The first deck landing of a jet fighter occurred aboard HMS *Ocean* in December 1945, but it was several years before operational squadrons could be deployed. By the outbreak of the Korean War in 1950, the British and American navies were still predominately equipped with piston engined

ABOVE: **The British "Colossus" class light fleet carriers proved ideal for postwar operations and several saw service during the Korean War. This is HMS *Ocean* in 1952 with a deckload of Sea Furies and Fireflies.** *via L.Marriott*

LEFT: **HMCS *Bonaventure*, an ex-British light fleet carrier converted to the ASW role for the Canadian Navy in the 1960s.** *via L.Marriott*

aircraft but, under the impetus of war, the introduction of jet fighters and strike aircraft was accelerated. However, there were a number of problems to be solved before the operation of jet aircraft from carriers could become routine. The new aircraft were larger and heavier than their predecessors but their initial acceleration was sluggish, so that a rolling take-off was not feasible, and the then standard hydraulic catapult was not powerful enough. When landing on, pilots had been traditionally guided onto the deck by a batsman who stood on a precarious platform at the side of the deck but this method was not suited to the jets with their higher approach speeds. Finally, in the event of a piston-engined aircraft missing the arrester wires, a steel safety net was rigged amidships which was caught the aircraft and prevented it running into other aircraft parked on the forward half of the flightdeck. However, this was never completely satisfactory and aircraft often overran the barrier with disastrous results, a situation which was much worse given the volatility of the early jet fuels.

Despite having a much smaller carrier fleet than their American cousins, it was the Royal Navy which came up

ABOVE: **HMCS *Huron* was a "Tribal" class destroyer completed in 1943 and earned a distinguished war record. In the postwar era she was converted to a fleet escort equipped with a dedicated anti-aircraft battery and twin Squid anti-submarine mortars aft.** *via L.Marriott*

ABOVE RIGHT: **A Grumman TBF-1 Avenger about to land on the deck of an Essex class carrier.** *via L. Marriott*

RIGHT: **The might of the US Navy on display at San Diego, the major facility on the American western seaboard. In the foreground are the carriers *George Washington, John C. Stennis, Dwight D. Eisenhower* and *Theodore Roosevelt*, while in the background is the USS *Enterprise* and major amphibious warfare vessels.** *via L. Marriott*

RIGHT: **The mirror landing sight. A British invention which gave visual guidance to pilots approaching a carrier for landing.** *via L.Marriott*

BELOW: **HMS *Victorious* was the only British wartime carrier to be modernized for the operation of jet aircraft by the addition of steam catapults and a fully angled deck.** *via L.Marriott*

Jet Aircraft at Sea

Jet aircraft were first flown from ships at the end of World War II, when the technology was in its infancy. As early jets such as Vampires were tested, it soon became apparent that larger carriers were needed to accommodate the longer take-off and landing of the new jet aircraft. During the 1950s jet aircraft took over from piston-engined aircraft, and a new generation of large carriers entered service. Today, the most advanced naval fighter aircraft, and the only one with variable geometry, is the US Grumman F-14 Tomcat. Take-off from the carrier deck is with the aid of a catapult, and it is landed using an arrestor. V/STOL (Vertical/Short Take-off) fixed-wing fighters, such as the Sea Harrier used by the Royal Navy's Fleet Air Arm, require a smaller take-off and landing area, often aided by a ski-jump at the end of the deck runway. The full range of jet aircraft types making up the wing on the largest US carriers, the "Nimitz" class, in addition to the F-14, includes McDonnell-Douglas F/A-18 Hornet multi-purpose fighters, Grumman A-6E Intruder attack aircraft as well as the electronic warfare EA-6B Prowler/KA-6D tanker variants and the Grumman E-2C Hawkeye EW aircraft (the only carrier-borne airborne early warning aircraft in service). Other navies with large carriers, such as the Russians and French, have developed their own range of naval jet aircraft.

with the solution to all of these problems. The necessary energy to accelerate and launch heavy aircraft was found by harnessing the immense power put out by the ship's boilers in a new steam catapult. To assist pilots of high performance aircraft making an approach to land, a stabilized mirror landing sight was developed which provided a constant visual reference, by night and day, so that the pilot was instantly aware of his position relative to the correct angle of approach. However the invention which perhaps most revolutionized carrier operations was also the most simple. It was Captain Cambell of the Royal Navy who first suggested that the axis of the flightdeck be offset by a few degrees to port, and in fact the first experiments were conducted simply by painting the appropriate line on the otherwise unmodified HMS *Triumph*. The most important effect of this arrangement was that an aircraft which failed to catch the arrester wires simply accelerated away and became airborne again for another landing attempt. There was no need for a safety barrier and, as a bonus, the ship could be ranging aircraft for catapult launches while landing operations were being conducted.

The ideal offset for an angled deck was at least 10 degrees, but this required a substantial modification the

form of a flightdeck extension along the port side of the ship and only three British carriers were completely modified in this way. These were the *Ark Royal, Hermes* (completed 1960) and also HMS *Victorious*, the only one of the wartime fleet carriers to be completely modernized; plans to modernize the others were dropped partly because of cost, but also because most of them were in too poor a condition resulting from hasty repairs to battle damage during World War II. It was, therefore, left to the US Navy to make the most of these inventions and many of the "Essex" class carriers were progressively modernized to incorporate full angled decks, steam catapults and the latest radar and electronic gear. The three "Midway" class carriers were also fully modified, but in 1955 the Americans launched the first of the 55,000 super-carriers which were designed from the start to make the most of the angled-deck layout and were provided with hangars capable of accommodating the largest naval aircraft then projected. The success of this design can be gauged from the fact that all subsequent US aircraft carriers have been built to the same basic plan, although with obvious variations in equipment and armament, and some increase in overall dimensions.

Perhaps the most dramatic change to be incorporated was the adoption of nuclear-powered propulsion machinery which was installed the USS *Enterprise*, commissioned in 1961. In fact the *Enterprise* was not the first US surface warship to be nuclear-powered, this distinction going the missile-armed cruiser USS *Long Beach* which entered service in 1961. Subsequently a total of eight further nuclear-powered cruisers ("Bainbridge," "Truxton," "California" and "West Virginia" classes) were built from 1960 to 1980 but most new warship construction used more

Nuclear Power

The potential of nuclear power for submarines was recognized soon after the end of World War II, and first used in the 1950s. The nuclear-propelled submarine is essentially driven by steam generated by the atomic energy (uranium) in the submarine's reactor. The steam drives the main turbine which is connected through gears by a shaft to the propeller. Although offering great advantages in range, endurance and speed, both the internal machinery and the propeller in nuclear submarines are noisy, particularly at speed, and can be detected at great distances. The cost of building nuclear-powered vessels means that only a handful of countries can afford to build or have a strategic requirement for them — USA, Russia, Britain, France and China. The development of nuclear power for surface ships was slower. The US Navy's first nuclear-propelled warship was the cruiser USS *Long Beach*, completed in 1961, followed shortly afterward by the first carrier, USS *Enterprise*, launched three years later. Although the overall cost of building *Enterprise* was estimated to be twice that of a conventional oil-fueled aircraft carrier, her almost limitless range and increased aviation fuel capacity make her comparatively cheap to operate and the later "Nimitz" class of carriers was also nuclear-propelled. Russia also operates nuclear-powered carriers and the nuclear-powered "Kirov" class battlecruisers, and France is introducing nuclear-powered carriers.

conventional propulsion systems. Within both political and defense circles there was considerable debate about the desirability and efficiency of nuclear propulsion, and consequently the next four carriers — of the "Kittyhawk" and "John F. Kennedy" classes — laid down after the *Enterprise* used traditional steam machinery. However, with the USS *Nimitz* and all subsequent carriers, nuclear propulsion was again adopted, and consequently these ships have an unlimited steaming endurance although their actual operational capacity depends on embarking enough stores, provisions, fuel and armament to maintain a community of over 5,000 crew and operate an air group of 80 or more aircraft and helicopters. The US Navy currently has available nine nuclear-powered carriers (CVN) as well as three "Kittyhawk" class carriers, although the latter will be replaced when CVN-76 (USS *Ronald Regan*) is completed in 2002 and CVN-77 in 2008. The latter will be completed to a modified design incorporating new electromagnetic catapults.

The only other nation to currently deploy a nuclear-powered aircraft carrier is France, which commissioned the 36,000-ton *Charles de Gaulle* in 2000. This can carry up to 40 aircraft and helicopters, and is initially equipped with a group of Super Etendard strike aircraft but these will be replaced by the Mach 2 Rafale multi-role fighter from 2002 onward. Previously the Marine Nationale had operated two 30,000-ton conventional carriers, *Clemenceau* and *Foch*, which dated from the early 1960s, but these were decommissioned in 1997 and 2000 respectively.

Propulsion Systems
(Gas-Turbine, Electric, Diesel)

Diesel propulsion systems were first used before World War II and are still used for smaller surface ships although pure diesels for large ships are not popular with many navies, such as the US Navy and the Royal Navy, because of their noisiness. Larger ships can use a combination of diesel and gas-turbine propulsion (CODOG), the diesels offering a boost during cruising. Gas-turbine (GT) propulsion systems have been developed more recently, and are becoming the most popular method of propulsion for faster warships. They have the advantage of low-manning, easy maintenance and more compact layout. The reduced underwater noise is particularly advantageous for anti-submarine operations. Disadvantages are that they need to be changed regularly for servicing, and that the requirement for large air intakes, and to expel large amounts of hot gases, can constrain ship design. Since World War II, diesel-electric systems, because of their cost and size, have tended to be used only for specialist surface ships, although their quiet running and sensitivity to low speeds means they have potential to back up GT systems on warships. Conventional submarines, however, use electric motors powered by batteries to rotate the propeller, with a diesel generator used to charge the batteries. Diesel-electric submarines are actually quieter in the water than nuclear-propelled submarines but are limited by needing fresh air to recharge batteries, an operation that can effectively be carried out only by resurfacing or snorkeling at low speeds.

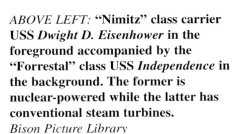

ABOVE LEFT: **"Nimitz" class carrier USS *Dwight D. Eisenhower* in the foreground accompanied by the "Forrestal" class USS *Independence* in the background. The former is nuclear-powered while the latter has conventional steam turbines.**
Bison Picture Library

LEFT: **The first large American carriers to be built after World War II were the four ships of the "Forrestal" class which were launched in the mid-1950s. These were designed to take full advantage of the British-invented angled deck and steam catapult, both of these features being clearly visible in this view of the USS *Saratoga*.**
Bison Picture Library

Missiles: Ship-to-Ship

A wide range of ship-to-ship missiles have been developed for today's navies. Most skim the sea and have active radar or infra-red (IR) homing. A large warship is extremely vulnerable to this attack, being relatively bulky and slow-moving and presenting a large IR/radar profile. One of the most widely used is the Russian P-15 cruise missile with a range of 50 miles. Another proven cruise missile is the US AGM-84 Harpoon with a maximum range of 75 miles and a maximum warhead of 500lb. Sea-skimming missiles are extremely effective, being difficult to pick up over the water and striking the vessel where it is vulnerable, in the hull. The AM-39 Exocet missile is perhaps the most widely used sea-skimming missile, with a range of 30 miles and a 350lb warhead. It proved its worth in the Iran-Iraq war, achieving a 90% hit rate, and the Falklands War when an aircraft-fired Exocet sank HMS *Sheffield* even though the warhead failed to explode. Other similar missiles include the British Sea Eagle with a range up to 70 miles and the Franco-Italian Otomat, using active-radar homing and with a "fire and update" system effective up to 100 miles. Smaller but effective missiles include the British Sea Skua with a range up to 10 miles and a 325lb warhead and the US Navy SH-60B Seahawk.

The great postwar build-up of western navies from the late 1940s onward was, of course, due to the threat posed by Soviet forces in the Cold War era. However, the Soviet navy had no tradition of carrier operations and instead concentrated on building powerful surface ships armed with long-range surface-to-surface missiles. They did not enter seriously into the field of naval aviation until 1967 when the first of two large 18,000-ton helicopter-carrying cruisers, *Leningrad* and *Moscow*, entered service. These were intended purely as anti-submarine vessels but they were followed in the 1970 and early 1980s by four 37,000-ton "Kiev" class aircraft carriers, which operate a mix of ASW helicopters and Yak-36 "Forger" vertical take-off jet fighters. A full angled deck was fitted, with a towering island superstructure offset to starboard. However, unlike western carriers, the foredeck was not part of the flightdeck and carried an extensive armament of guns and missiles. With the end of the cold war all of these were laid up and abandoned, although one has now been sold to India where it will be substantially rebuilt before entering service. Russia's final effort to enter the world of blue-water carrier forces was the 55,000 "Kuznetzov" class, of which two were laid down in the mid-1980s but only the name ship was completed, in 1991. The *Admiral Flota Sovietskogo*

RIGHT: **A bow shot of HMS *Invincible* showing the ski jump ramp which enabled the Sea Harriers to take-off with substantially heavier weapon and fuel loads.** *via L.Marriott*

Sojuza Kuznetsov (to give the ship's full name) was similar in size and layout to the American "Forrestal" class of the 1950s but an obvious difference was the ski jump ramp on the bow. The air group was much more potent than that of the preceding "Kiev" class ships, comprising supersonic Sukhoi Su-27 (or Su-33) jet fighters and Sukhoi Su-25 strike aircraft. This ship clearly indicated that the Russians intended to match the US Navy in the worldwide deployment of carrier task forces, but the collapse of the Russian economy has meant that no funds are available for further construction and even the *Kuznetsov* has only seen limited service.

The Soviet Navy was the first to deploy an operational VTOL fighter at sea but this development was closely echoed by the Royal Navy, which had lost its fixed-wing carrier capability (for rather dubious political motives) with the retirement of the *Ark Royal* in 1978. Fortunately the new 20,000-ton "Invincible" class "through-deck cruisers," the first of which commissioned in 1980, were capable of embarking and operating a naval version of the Harrier vertical take-off fighter which had been in service with the RAF since 1970. Redesignated an aircraft carrier as soon as it was politically expedient to do so, HMS *Invincible* showed her worth in the 1982 Falklands War. A total of three "Invincible" class are currently in service and will soldier on for at least another decade before being replaced by two new 40,000-ton "Future Aircraft Carriers" which will probably embark the US-developed JSF (Joint Strike Fighter). The success of the Sea Harrier (also adopted by the US Marines as the AV-8A/B) prompted several navies to build small aircraft carriers capable of operating this versatile aircraft. Spain built the 17,000-ton *Principe de Asturias* which commissioned in 1988 and this led to an order from Thailand for the 11,500-ton *Chakri Narubet* which was delivered in 1997. Italy built the 13,800-ton *Guiseppe Garibaldi* in the early 1980s, and plans a larger 22,000-ton carrier to be completed in 2007. Interestingly, almost all of these small carriers are powered by gas -turbines which, together diesel engines, now power the majority of the world's surface warships.

Apart from the large US aircraft carriers, nuclear power was not widely applied in surface craft but it did find a ready home aboard the submarine. Ever since the invention of a viable underwater craft, the world's navies had dreamed of a submarine which could operate continuously underwater, independent of an air supply for its engines or crew. This concept was finally made possible by the development of a nuclear powerplant, but its application to a submarine was very much the work of one man, Admiral H. G. Rickover of the US Navy. Following the formulation of a requirement for such a craft, it was his drive, vision and

ABOVE: **USS *Richard Russell* was the last of 37 "Sturgeon" class SSNs launched between 1967 and 1975.** *TRH Pictures/US Navy*

RIGHT: **USS *Portsmouth* a "Los Angeles" class SSN.** *TRH Pictures/General Dynamics*

BELOW: **USS *Queenfish* (SSN-651) a "Sturgeon class" SSN launched in 1966.** *TRH Pictures*

ABOVE: **USS *Grayback* (SSG-574), completed in 1958, was a conventionally powered submarine designed to carry the Regulus II SSN. These were housed in the bulbous forward hangar but could only be fired when the submarine was on the surface. *Grayback* is seen entering San Diego harbor.** *TRH Pictures/US Navy*

RIGHT: **The British "Oberon" class diesel-powered patrol submarines were completed in the 1960s, although the bulbous sonar housing was a later addition. Despite the relatively conventional hull form, they were remarkably quiet when running submerged.** *via L.Marriott*

determination which led to the commissioning in 1955 of the USS *Nautilus* as the word's first nuclear-powered submarine. Subsequently this vessel clearly demonstrated the potential of such a combination by steaming over 150,000 miles on one reactor, refueling and conducting several long distance voyages while deeply submerged. The most spectacular of these was from Pearl Harbor in the Pacific to Portland in the United Kingdom via the geographic north pole by sailing under the Arctic icepack. Once the concept was proved, the British and US navies concentrated almost exclusively on nuclear-powered submarines, but there was still a place for the conventional diesel-electric submarine which had undergone considerable development since the end of the war in 1945.

Early postwar submarine development was almost entirely based on the technology evolved from captured German U-boats, particularly the streamlined Type XXI. The US Navy subsequently converted many of the wartime "Balao" and "Tench" class boats under the Guppy program, — this being an acronym for Greater Underwater Propulsive Power. Under this scheme, selected submarines were fitted with a new efficient battery system giving greater electrical capacity to drive new, more powerful, electric motors. The hull casing was completely rebuilt to

offer a more streamlined form while all guns and other external fittings were removed. Updated sonar and radar equipment was fitted and, as modified, these boats could make 15 knots underwater. The Guppy program was carried out between 1947 and 1952 and six new submarines, the "Tang" class, were also completed in the early 1950s. In addition to incorporating all the Guppy modifications from the start, they also introduced a new type of diesel engine which, unfortunately, turned out to be unreliable and was eventually replaced by conventional units. The US Navy also converted two older submarines, and built three more (two diesel-electric and one nuclear-powered) to carry the Regulus nuclear-tipped cruise missile. This was much less sophisticated than modern cruise missiles, and was soon to be supplanted by the infinitely more powerful ballistic missiles. However, the most significant of the US diesel-electric submarines was the USS *Albacore*, completed in December 1953. This was the first submarine to adopt the bulbous whale-shaped hull now common in modern submarines, both conventionally and nuclear-powered. Apart from a few specialized and experimental submarines, no diesel-electric submarines were built for the USN after the late 1950s, all subsequent development concentrating on nuclear powered submarines following the unqualified success of the USS *Nautilus*.

British submarine development closely followed that of the US Navy. In the immediate postwar period many of the wartime "T" class boats were substantially modified. There hulls were lengthened to allow a greater battery capacity and the hull was streamlined with some boats sporting a large and conspicuous "sail" in place of the conventional low profile conning tower. The larger "A" class, under construction at the end of the war, were all similarly modified. As these older boats became due for replacement the highly successful Porpoise/Oberon classes were put into production between 1955 and 1963. Considered by many to be the finest conventional submarines ever built, they displaced 2,500 tons underwater and could make 17 knots when submerged while they were capable of almost totally silent running at low speeds

While the US pressed ahead with nuclear power, the British attempted to develop the German Walter system and built two submarines (*Excalibur* and *Explorer*) powered by HTP turbines. HTP stood for high test peroxide, which was a very volatile substance and dangerous to handle. One British submarine, HMS *Sidon*, was destroyed in an accidental detonation of one of the experimental HTP torpedoes she was carrying. Although the system had some promise, by the time the first boat, *Explorer*, commenced trials in 1957, it was overshadowed by the demonstrated potential of nuclear power, and after a period of trials and employment as high-speed targets, both were scrapped in the mid-1960s.

In the meantime, the US Navy had pressed ahead rapidly with nuclear-powered submarines. The first operational boats were the relatively small (2,800 tons submerged) "Skate" class completed in 1957-58. At the same time, the 6,700-ton *Triton* was completed and she was powered by not one, but two, nuclear reactors. She was designed as a high-speed radar picket to operate with the surface fleet, a role which became redundant with the development of carrier-based airborne early warning systems although she did hit the headlines in 1960 on completion of the first submerged circumnavigation of the world, a 36,000-mile trip. All of these submarines had relatively conventional, if streamlined, hull forms, but the 3,500-ton (submerged) "Skipjack" class commissioned from 1959 onward featured the high-performance teardrop-hull shape pioneered by the USS *Albacore*. Subsequently US nuclear-powered attack submarines evolved from this basic design, each slightly larger than its predecessor and introducing new and sophisticated sonar arrays as these were developed. Following the "Skipjack" class were the 14 boats of the "Thresher" class (4,300 tons submerged) completed during the 1960s, and no fewer than 37 "Sturgeon" class vessels (4,650 tons submerged) were commissioned up to 1975. All of these have now been retired and the current attack submarine fleet comprises almost totally the 51 6,900-ton (submerged) "Los Angeles," class which entered service from 1976 onward. These are optimized for operation under the Arctic icepack and carry Tomahawk sub-launched cruise missiles as well as ADCAP (advance capability) torpedoes. Their successor was intended to be the class based on the SSN-21 *Seawolf* but these 9,000-ton boats, reputedly capable of running silently at 20 knots submerged, proved to be too expensive and only three will be completed.

Once again, Britain followed the US lead and its first nuclear-powered attack submarine, HMS *Dreadnought* was fitted with a US-designed reactor system. Completed in 1963, she was followed by five similar boats built between 1962 and 1971. One of these, HMS *Conqueror*, was responsible for the sinking of the Argentinean cruiser *General Belgrano*, using conventional torpedoes, during the 1982 Falklands War. The succeeding "Swiftsure" and "Trafalgar" classes built in the 1970s and 80s were slightly larger with a more refined hull form. These boats remain in service and are armed with the Spearfish heavyweight guided torpedo and some are modified to fire Tomahawk cruise missiles. In the next decade the 7,200-ton "Astute" class will enter service and as the earlier "S" class boats are retired.

ABOVE RIGHT: **A British "Trafalgar" class nuclear-powered submarine enters harbor. These boats have recently been upgraded to carry the Tomahawk sub-launched cruise missile.** *L.Marriott*

RIGHT: **A "Swiftsure" class nuclear-powered attack submarine (SSN) of the Royal Navy.** *via L.Marriott*

ABOVE: **HMS** *Resolution* was one of five British strategic missile submarines commissioned between 1967 and 1969. Armed with 16 Polaris A3 nuclear missiles with a range of 2,500 nautical miles, they served until 1996 when the larger Trident-armed "Vanguard" class SSBNs entered service. *via L.Marriott*

ABOVE RIGHT: Britain's nuclear deterrent force is now comprised of the four "Vanguard" class SSBNs. The name ship is shown here after being rolled out in an almost complete state prior to launching in 1993. Despite the awesome power of the 16 Trident ballistic missiles, these boats are still armed with conventional torpedo tubes, the opening for which can be seen on the side of the bow casing. *via L.Marriott*

RIGHT: **HMS** *Dreadnought* was Britain's first nuclear-powered submarine. *Bison Picture Library*

The ultimate development of the submarine as a weapon system came about when they were adapted to carry strategic nuclear ballistic missiles. The first of these, USS *George Washington*, commissioned in 1959, and her design was basically similar to the contemporary "Skipjack" class except that the hull was lengthened amidships by 130ft to provide the space for 16 vertical launch silos, each holding a 1,500-mile range Polaris missile. Thus equipped, the submarine could slip away and hide in the depths of the ocean, ready to launch its missiles at a variety of targets at a moment's notice. The combination of submarine and ballistic missile has proved to be the ultimate in deterrent forces and they were deployed in large numbers; the original Polaris A-1 missile was developed into the A-3 with greater range and multiple warheads. The current US strategic missile submarine force centers on 18 18,750-ton "Ohio" class submarines which each carry 24 Trident missiles with a range of up to 6,500 miles, while each missile can deploy up to 12 100-kiloton independently targetable nuclear warheads. The destructive power of just one of these submarines defies imagination.

Once again, Britain followed in the wake of their American cousins, commissioning four "Resolution" class nuclear submarines armed with 16 Polaris missiles in the late 1960s. These have now been retired and have been replaced by four 15,900-ton "Vanguard" class SSBNs which commissioned between 1993 and 1999. These are armed with 16 Trident D5 strategic missiles with a similar capability to those deployed by the US Navy. In fact, in both cases the full potential of the missiles have been downgraded by the various Strategic Arms Reduction Treaties (START) which limit the numbers of warheads and missiles which can be deployed. The future is perhaps indicated by the new "Virginia" class, due to enter service with the US Navy in 2004. Although classified as attack submarines, these boats will carry multiple cruise missiles launched from vertical silos as well as advanced torpedoes discharged from four bow tubes. Displacing 7,800 tons submerged, they will be capable of underwater speeds in excess of 30 knots and will be equipped with the latest sonars for anti-submarine warfare. Four have been ordered to date, with a possible requirement for up to 30 in next two decades.

The build-up of the US and British submarine fleets was almost entirely in due to the increase in Soviet naval

ABOVE RIGHT AND RIGHT: **USS *Michigan* (SSBN-727) the second "Ohio" class to be completed. The massive length of the hull, which houses 16 ballistic missiles, is clearly shown.** *TRH Pictures/US Navy; TRH Pictures/General Dynamics*

FAR LEFT: **Russian "Foxtrot" class submarine with "Kashin" class destroyer in background.** *TRH/US Navy*

LEFT: **USS *Phoenix* (SSN-702), a "Los Angeles" class attack submarine.** *TRH Pictures/US Navy*

ABOVE: **USS *Chopper* (SS-342) was a modernized wartime-built "Balao" class submarine. This was known as the "Guppy" conversion. Overhead is a Lockheed P-3 Orion ASW aircraf during an exercise in the Gulf of Mexico.** *Bison Picture Library*

strength in the postwar years, and at the height of the Cold War the two superpowers played a cat and mouse game under the surface of the world's oceans and icepacks. During World War II the Soviets had built mostly small coastal submarines, which achieved few successes. However, they were quick to adopt the German technology which fell into their hands at the end of the war and the "Whiskey" class conventional submarines, which began to appear in large numbers from 1950 onward, were obviously based on the German Type XXI. This and the similar "Romeo" class displaced around 1,200-1,500 tons submerged and were armed with 21-inch torpedoes. A large 2,200-ton ocean-going submarine ("Zulu" class) was produced from 1954 onward. As Russia lagged behind the United States in development of nuclear-powered boats, their first stragegic missile submarines were conventionally powered and the missile launch silos, typically only two or three per boat, were stacked vertically behind the sail. An example of this approach was the 2,800-ton "Golf" class

which appeared in 1961 and was instantly recognizable by the long conning tower which enclosed three SS-N-4 or -5 nuclear missiles. These had a relatively limited range of 300-700 miles. The first nuclear-powered strategic missile submarines was the "Hotel" class, which entered service from 1958 onward, but again only carried three SS-N-5 missiles. They were very similar in outline to the conventional "Golf" class but were almost twice the displacement.

The Soviets did not have anything which really matched the American *George Washington* and later SSBNs until the 10,000-ton "Yankee" class was introduced in 1967. These carried 16 SS-N-6 missiles with a range of 1,500 miles, similar to that of the Polaris used by the US and British navies. The next strategic missile submarine was the "Delta," of which the first was completed in 1972. These were designed to carry the 4,200-mile range SS-N-8 "Sawfly" missile, which was longer than the SS-N-6. The longer missile silos were enclosed in a distinctive hump-back casing aft of the conning tower, and this made the "Delta" class instantly recognizable. They were built in considerable numbers and several variants, culminating the current "Delta IV" which is armed with the SS-N-23 "Skiff" three-stage missile with a range of 4,500 miles and carrying up to 10 MIRV 100-kiloton nuclear warheads. The ultimate Russian submarine, and the largest submersible ever built, is the monster 26,500-ton (submerged) "Typhoon" class, which entered service in great secrecy in 1981. These are actually twin-hulled submarines although this is hidden by the streamlined casing and the missile

TOP: **Russian "Victor III" class SSN.** *TRH Pictures/US Navy*

ABOVE: **USS *Buffalo* (SSN-715), a "Los Angeles" class attack submarine launched in 1992.** *TRH Pictures/US Navy*

silos for 20 "Sturgeon" missiles are all in the forward section with the conning tower set after. Each of the hulls has its own nuclear powerplant.

With each side deploying numerous strategic missile submarines, their location, tracking and destruction if required, became the highest priority of all major navies. The most effective way of doing this was with fast nuclear-powered attack submarines optimized for the ASW role — such as the British "Trafalgar" and the US "Los Angeles" classes. The Russians, rather than develop and improve a single design, introduced a confusing variety of submarines

over the years. The first was the 4,000-ton "November" class, which commissioned between 1958 and 1963. Then there was the "Victor" class from 1967 onward. These were built in several variants and were very fast, if somewhat noisy, underwater. The subsequent "Alpha" class was slightly smaller and was reputedly capable of 40 knots submerged. However, the overall design was not an operational success and all have been withdrawn, although some two dozen "Victor IIs" are still available.

In the early 1960s, the Soviet Navy began deploying large numbers of jet-powered surface-to-surface missiles — with ranges from 150 to 300 miles. Several of these, such as the SS-N-3 "Shaddock," were adapted for launching from submarines, although initially only when surfaced. More modern boats are equipped with the more sophisticated cruise missiles such as the SS-N-21 "Sampson," which carries a 200-kiloton nuclear warhead over a range of 1,600 miles at Mach 0.7. These now arm the "Sierra" and "Akula" classes which displace around 7,000-9,000 tons. The largest of the cruise missile submarines is the "Oscar" class of which one, the *Kursk*, hit the headlines in 2000 when it was lost with all hands during a live-firing exercise. These boats are massive, displacing up to 13,500 tons submerged and are armed with 24 SS-N-19 "Shipwreck" cruise missiles with a range of 300 miles and intended mainly for the anti-ship role. Russia has not neglected the development of the conventional diesel-powered submarine and the "Kilo" class, dating from 1979, has been particularly successful and has been exported to several countries including China, India, Iran and Poland.

Of course, the submarine is not only deployed by the superpowers, and both China and France have built their own nuclear-powered strategic and attack submarines. Conventional submarines have also become very sophisticated and Germany, which began building successors to the wartime U-boats in 1955, is now a major player in the

ABOVE: **Russian "Oscar" class SSGN. Note the housing for a towed array sonar on the stern.** *TRH Pictures/US Navy*

Missiles: Surface-to-Air

Surface-to-air missiles (SAMs) were developed for naval ships in order to protect themselves against air attack at a distance greater than a few kilometers surrounding the attacked vessel(s). The most sophisticated system is the US Navy's Aegis, comprising computer-controlled multi-function phased-array radar, a fire-control system, SM-2 SAMs, magazines, automatic loading systems and VLS (vertical launch systems). The most widely used SAMs are the US Navy SM-2ER/MR (Standard Missile type 2, Extended/Medium Range) and the Royal Navy Sea Dart. The SM-2, at Mach 2.5, can engage targets up to 137km away, although a sea-skimming target would have to be engaged closer. Sea Dart can engage targets up to a distance of only 25 miles but can engage sea-skimming missiles and ships. Closer-range weapons are also required, the most widely used being Sea Sparrow, Sea Wolf and Crotale. The US Navy's semi-active homing Sea Sparrow is an adaptation of the Sparrow AAM and has a maximum range of 10 miles. Crotale is an adaptation of a land SAM and has a range of eight miles. The Royal Navy's Sea Wolf is the only system specifically designed for ship AAW defence. It has radio/TV command and differential radar tracking and has proved its effectiveness in downing aircraft, sea-skimming missiles and even shells fired from naval guns up to a range of three miles. Hand-held missiles are also used for close-in defence, the US Stinger, with a range up to 5,000 yards, and the British Javelin being the most widely used.

export market with the new Type 212 and 214. These are designed to take advantage of new air independent propulsion (AIP) systems which use devices such as fuel cells and Stirling cycle engines to provide sustained underwater power over much longer periods than the conventional battery systems. The Swedish "Gotland" class, which was completed in 1997, was the first to be designed from scratch to use AIP but throughout the world several navies are now experimenting with this system which can give an underwater endurance of up to 14 days at slow speeds.

The massive leap in submarine technology, dating from the end of World War II, immediately required similar advances in ASW technology, and much of what was developed during the war became obsolete overnight, particularly with the advent of the nuclear submarine. ASW warships needed to be faster and to carry weapons which could engage submarines as soon as they were detected and identified, and the range at which this occurred constantly increased as new and more sophisticated sonar system were introduced. The disadvantage of a simple depth charge is that the surface ship has to be directly over the submarine before it can attack, and so during World War II ahead-throwing weapons (ATW), such as "Hedgehog" and "Squid," were developed, with ranges of around 250 yards. The latter was particularly significant as it was the first ASW weapon to be completely integrated with the sonar system to determine the exact moment of firing. After the war it was developed into the Limbo system which had a range of up 1,000 yards. However, sonars such as the British Type 184 and the American SQS-4 introduced in the 1950s were capable of detecting submarines at ranges in

203

Anti-Submarine Warfare

Anti-submarine warfare (ASW) has developed apace with the growth of the submarine as today's most powerful capital ship. The development of nuclear power for submarine propulsion after the war meant that the underwater endurance of the submarine and the speed at which it could travel became vastly improved. ASW became increasingly focused on the submarine at depth. During the Cold War the USA and USSR established enormous chains of fixed underwater listening sonar installations at key points off enemy coasts, ports and well-known shipping routes (the US system is known as SOSUS), connected to a shore-listening station by wire or radio. The USA also uses mobile underwater sonar arrays dropped by aircraft or towed by ship. Both types of sonar are intended to pick up the noise made by a submarine when moving. Long-range patrols using ASW aircraft and even satellite detection are used, and fixed-wing aircraft or helicopters can drop active or passive sonobuoys. Aircraft can also carry a Magnetic Anomaly Detector (MAD) which will register at short range the presence of the submarine and sophisticated radar which will detect a submarine on the surface. If a submarine were to engage a surface enemy by torpedo strike the conventional defences of keeping the threatened shipping close together, moving at maximum speed and maneuvering to create sonic confusion and using aircraft cover still apply. Theoretically, submarines could themselves be used to track and engage enemy submarines although the practice of this would not be easy.

LEFT: **The Royal Navy converted many wartime destroyers to fast anti-submarine frigates during the early 1950s as a stopgap measure until new frigates could be built. HMS *Ulster* was launched in 1942 and converted to a Type 15 frigate between 1953 and 1956.** *via L.Marriott*

205

Underwater Weapons

Postwar, the use of underwater weapons continued the developments of World War II. Mines, either acoustic, magnetic, seismic or pressure-activated are a long-standing defence against shipping and submarines, although are less effective in deep water. The standard explosive charge ranges from 220lb to 1,000lb and is sufficient to disable a destroyer or frigate. A sonar-activated mine which fires a torpedo when it has locked on to a target has also been developed. The other major underwater weapon is the torpedo. The submarine or heavyweight torpedo has a 533mm diameter and weighs about 3,400lb, with a 420-550lb warhead. Although torpedoes have developed over the years the basic design has remained remarkably consistent. The British Mk VIII torpedo, developed before World War II, was still in use in the 1980s and was used by the submarine HMS *Conqueror* to sink *General Belgrano*. Modern torpedoes home in on the target at speeds up to 45kts, and are programed to turn around and search for the target if the first run misses. Lightweight torpedoes have also been developed, particularly for ASW, which can be launched from aircraft (including helicopters) or surface vessels and which again home in on the submarine. These include the British Stingray missile and the US Mk 46, as well as a range of missile-launched torpedoes. Depth charges are also used by a number of navies as part of ASW, and today can be fitted with active homing devices and nuclear explosive charges.

excess of 10,000 yards and some form of ASW weapon which could reach out to such ranges was required. The answer was to provide a rocket-powered guided missile which could carry an anti-submarine homing torpedo out to the target area. Once released the torpedo would then use its own active honing system to attack the submarine. The British adopted the Australian-designed Ikara missile system, first introduced aboard the destroyer HMS *Bristol* in 1967, while the US Navy went for the ASROC system from 1960 onward. This featured an eight-cell missile launcher, although in the past decade a vertical launch system has been developed. Although these systems were very effective within their operational range, they could not cope with every scenario and a much more flexible system turned out to the use of a helicopter carrying depth charges or homing torpedoes. This was pioneered by the British in the mid-1950s with the MATCH (Manned Torpedo-Carrying Helicopter) program, while the Americans experimented with the DASH (Destroyer Anti-Submarine Helicopter) which was an unmanned drone. However, the manned helicopter proved much more effective and was also capable of carrying out many other roles and consequently there are now few major surface warships which do not carry at least one helicopter.

But what of the ships needed to carry all of these weapons and associated equipment? At the end of the war, both US and British navies had destroyers, frigates and escort vessels in abundance, but few of these would be effective against the new breeds of high-tech submarines then being developed. As the Cold War loomed at the end of the 1940s, one immediate solution adopted by both navies was to take many of the wartime destroyers, which had the necessary speed, strip them of the original armament and install new weapons optimised for the ASW role.

The Royal Navy produced two conversions based on the standard Emergency Program destroyers. The most extensive and successful was the Type 16 in which the ship was completely rebuilt with greatly expanded superstructure amidships to house radar and sonar equipment and a Combat Information Center (CIC), while armament comprised two Limbo ASW mortars and a twin 4-inch gun for air defence. A simpler conversion was the Type 16, in which the basic destroyer profile and some of the armament

was retained, a new enclosed bridge was fitted and two Squid A/S mortars installed on the quarterdeck. The US Navy carried out a similar program and, in fact, some uncompleted "Gearing" class destroyers were subsequently commissioned in 1947 as the "Carpenter" class with one of the twin 5-inch mounts replaced by Weapon Alpha, the US equivalent to the British Limbo. A number of other "Gearing" class vessels were similarly converted. A more ambitious program was applied to large numbers of both "Sumner" and "Gearing" class destroyers under the FRAM (Fleet Repair and Modernization) program instituted in the late 1960s. The basic FRAM I scheme involved the removal of torpedo tubes and the after twin 5-inch gun mount, the overhaul and refurbishment of the main machinery, enlarged bridge structure, new sonar equipment and the ASROC weapon system. A total of 79 ships was modified to this standard while a further 52 underwent FRAM II which encompassed all the foregoing but added a flightdeck for DASH operation and a variable depth sonar (VDS) on the stern.

LEFT: **Russian "Papa" class SSGN.** *via TRH Pictures*

BELOW: **Many American wartime destroyers were subsequently converted to ASW escorts under the FRAM (Fleet Repair and Modernization) program of the 1950s and 1960s. This is USS *Sarsfield*, a Gearing FRAM II conversion. Note the ASW torpedo launchers forward, ASROC between the funnels and a flightdeck for the DASH drone aft.** *via L.Marriott*

The first completely new American ocean-going ASW warships turned out be the size of wartime cruisers and, as such, were far too large and expensive for widescale deployment. The 5,600 ton *Norfolk*, launched in 1951, was armed with eight 3-inch automatic guns and carried two Weapon Alpha. The ship was later used as testbed for the ASROC system. She was followed by four smaller "Mitscher" class ships in 1952, each armed with 5-inch guns and Weapon Alpha, and which were later modified to carry the DASH system. Construction of more conventional ASW escorts did not commence until the early 1950s due to the hundreds of wartime DEs still available. However the 1,280-ton "Dealey" class was armed with Weapon Alpha and ASW torpedoes, and several were also built for export.

The US frigate program continued with the "Bronstein" class commissioned in 1962 and the "Garcia" class completed from 1964 onward. The basic design was progressively developed to produce the 3,000-ton "Knox" class which was built in large numbers from 1968 onward. This was immediately recognizable by a distinctive "mack" which combined the functions of a mast and smokestack. These ships were designed from the start to carried a manned helicopter, as well as a comprehensive sonar suite and ASROC.

The next significant frigate design was the 2,750-ton "Oliver Hazard Perry" class, of which over 50 were built between 1975 and 1989 A further six were built for the Australian Navy (including two built in Australia) and others for Taiwan and Spain. The design of these ships was to a strict cost limit, which led to many compromises and partly accounted for their unusual profile with a single large superstructure block surmounted a squat funnel right aft and a single 3-inch gun amidships. Despite their small size, these ships pack a heavy punch with the Standard surface-to-air missiles and Harpoon anti-ship missiles in addition to a helicopter and a comprehensive ASW suite.

British postwar frigate development built on the great experience of ASW operations gained during World War II. A building program instituted in 1951 resulted in the Type 12 frigate, armed with twin Limbo and twin 4.5-inch guns. Particular attention was paid to the hull design in order to produce a ship with good seakeeping characteristics and also able to maintain high speeds in rough weather. The design later evolved into the "Rothesay" class, which incorporated a helicopter hangar and flightdeck aft. This in turn led to the highly successful 2,300-ton "Leander" class general-purpose frigate, of which 26 were built for the Royal Navy and many more were built in the UK and abroad for several other navies, including Australia, New

RIGHT: **A Harpoon antiship missile is fired from a US "Knox" class frigate. This missile has been widely adopted by Western navies and has a range of up to 100 miles.**
Bison Picture Library

ABOVE: **The 2,700-ton "Oliver Hazard Perry" class was built in greater numbers than any other postwar US frigate design. Shown here is the USS *John L.Hall* (FFG-32). This ship has proved popular with other navies with new examples being built by Australia and Taiwan, while ex-US Navy examples are now being passed on to other nations including Poland and Turkey.**
Bison Picture Library

RIGHT: **The American "Knox" class frigates were near contemporaries of the British "Leander" class although, at 4,000 tons full load displacement, they were somewhat larger. A distinguishing feature was the combined mast and smokestack, known as a "mack." DE1063 shown here is the USS *Reasoner*, one of several "Knox" class frigates updated by the addition a Sea Sparrow basic point defence missile system (BPDMS) on the stern.**
Bison Picture Library

Zealand, India and the Netherlands. Originally armed with the Limbo ASW weapon, some were later modified to carry the Ikara anti-submarine missile and the Exocet anti-ship missile, while others received the short-range, but highly lethal, Seawolf surface-to-air missile.

As part of the 1951 program a number of Type 61 aircraft direction and Type 41 anti-aircraft frigates were laid down using a similar hull to the Type 12, but were powered by diesel engines instead of conventional steam turbines. In addition, a number of small Type 14 "Blackwood" class frigates, armed solely for the ASW task, were also completed in the late 1950s. However, the construction of several separate frigate types was uneconomic and also could cause tactical problems. It was for this reason that all roles were combined into one general-purpose design which led to the "Leander" class.

The next frigate design, the Type 81 "Tribal" class, was the first to incorporate a gas-turbine as part of the main machinery. Initial trials with this form of propulsion had been carried out aboard converted Type 14, HMS *Exmouth*, and in the "Tribals" a single 7,500shp gas-turbine supplemented the standard 12,500shp steam turbine. The results obtained with operational gas-turbines led to the first all-gas-turbine major warship to enter service with a western navy, the Type 21 "Amazon" class frigates, which commissioned from 1974 onward (the distinction of the world's

RIGHT: **In the 1950s the Royal Navy commissioned the new Type 12 fast anti-submarine frigates. The second group was modified after completion with the addition of a hangar and flightdeck aft as seen in this fine shot of HMS *Yarmouth*. A single Limbo ASW mortar can be seen in a well aft of the flightdeck.** *via L. Marriott*

BELOW: **The "Leander" class frigates, which entered service from 1963 onward, introduced the concept of the general-purpose frigate capable of a variety of operational roles in addition to the basic ASW function. Picture shows HMS *Juno*, completed in 1967.** *via L. Marriott*

LEFT: **Russian "Modified Kashin" class destroyer.** *TRH Pictures/US DoD*

BELOW LEFT: **The Type 23 is the latest British frigate design, and in all some 16 of this class have been launched. The angled sides of the hangar, funnel and superstructure are a partial attempt at a stealth profile.** *L.Marriott*

first all-gas-turbine major warship goes to the Russian "Kashin" class destroyers dating back to the early 1960s. The 2,750-ton Type 21 was a fine-looking ship, but was initially lightly armed for its size, although this was addressed as all ships eventually received the Seacat surface-to-air and Exocet anti-ship missiles. Eight were built and most participated in the Falklands War where two (*Ardent* and *Antelope*) were lost to intense air attacks.

The last British specialized ASW frigate was the Type 22 "Broadsword" class, which entered service from 1978 onward. These had the distinction of being the first British ships built to all metric standards, and they were also the first major warship to rely almost entirely on guided missiles as the main armament (two single 40mm guns were also carried). Displacing some 3,500 tons, these were large ships and could carry two Lynx helicopters. They were built in two batches, the later Batch II being distinguished by a longer hull, but the ultimate development was the 4,200-ton Batch III, which incorporated the lessons of the Falklands war and mounted a 4.5-inch gun while the Exocets were replaced by the longer-ranged Harpoon anti-ship missile. The hangar and flightdeck was sized to accommodate a Sea King ASW helicopter or its replacement, the Merlin HA.1 which is due to become operational in 2003.

The latest British frigate is the Type 23 which has been in production since 1985. Optimized for the ASW role, it is still well able to defend itself with Seawolf missiles and a 4.5-inch gun, as well as carrying Harpoon missiles for the anti-ship role. However, its propulsion system is extremely flexible with Spey gas-turbines for cruising and high-speed, and a unique diesel-electric drive for quiet operations while carrying out ASW operations. Modern sonar technology has considerably developed the capabilities of passive sonar systems by using digital signal-processing techniques to filter out unwanted noises. The Type 23, in common with many other modern frigates (and submarines), is equipped with a towed array, which can be trailed several miles behind the ship and provides accurate range and bearing information without the submarine being aware that it has been detected. To make the best of this system, the ship's own machinery needs to be a quiet as possible and this

RIGHT: **Another "Kashin" class destroyer — the *Krasny Krym*.** *TRH Pictures/DoD/US Navy*

accounts for the choice of the CODLAG (combined diesel electric and gas-turbine) propulsion system. The last of 16 Type 23s was launched in May 2000 and is due to commission in 2002.

Russian efforts in the ASW field were mostly centered around various corvettes and small frigates, most intended for coastal work, but in 1970 they started building the 3,100-ton "Krivak" class frigates, which were very much the equal of their western contemporaries and were heavily armed with surface-to-surface and surface-to-air missiles, as well as the SS-N-14 "Silex" ASW missile with a a range of 30 miles. "Silex" could carry either a conventional homing torpedo or a five-kiloton nuclear warhead. The "Krivaks" were followed in the mid-1980s by the much larger 6,700-ton "Udaloy" class, which again was armed with the "Silex" ASW missile. A flightdeck and twin hangars aft can accommodate two Ka-27 "Helix" helicopters. Twelve of these were completed, but only one of the later "Udaloy IIs" was completed, in 1995.

In the postwar era the frigate was established principally as an anti-submarine vessel, although there was a trend to equip them for other roles, and some of the later examples, such as the Type 22 Batch IIIs, could almost be considered

215

to be cruisers. However, in most cases, even if missile-equipped, they were only able to defend *themselves* effectively against air attack, and the air defence of a task force began to fall to the destroyer. As with other types of warship, very few new destroyers were constructed immediately after the war, although the controversial British "Daring" class, completed 1952-54, were one notable exception. Armed with six 4.5-inch guns backed up by a radar-control high-angle fire-control system, they were as effective as many wartime cruisers in the anti-aircraft role. Otherwise the Royal Navy relied mainly on the "C" class emergency destroyers completed at the end of the war, and also numbers of "Battle" class destroyers, which also had an effective AA capability. Some of these, together with four "Weapon" class destroyers originally designed as fleet anti-submarine escorts (similar to the US "Carpenter" class) were converted to radar pickets. As already noted, many other wartime destroyers were converted to fast frigates.

The Royal Navy also retained a number of conventional gun cruisers in the postwar era. These also provided AA firepower for the fleet as well as being able to support amphibious landings (as was done in Korea), and provide the necessary space and communication facilities to act as force flagships when required. However, by the early 1960s most of them had been retired apart from the three "Tiger" class, which had originally been laid down as far back as 1941-42, but had been laid up incomplete at the end of the war. In 1955 work began to complete them to a revised design carrying fully automatic 6-inch and 3-inch guns and they were commissioned in this form some five years later. They were among the most advanced gun-armed cruiser ever built, but by the time they entered service, the guided missile was already taking over as the prime air defence weapon. In the late 1960s the "Tiger" class ships were converted to helicopter cruisers by the replacement of the after

ABOVE: **Russian "Kashin" class destroyer, the world's first all-gas-turbine-powered major warship.** *TRH Pictures*

LEFT: **In the later stages of their careers, several "Leander" class frigates were modernized by the addition of new weapons and sensors. This is HMS *Penelope* which was modified in 1981 to carry Exocet anti-ship missiles and additional Seacat short range SAMs, space for these being provide by the removal of the 4.5-inch twin mounting from the forecastle.** *via L. Marriott*

BELOW: Provorny **of the Russian "Kashin" class.** *TRH Pictures/US Navy*

ABOVE: The Canadian Navy built on their hard-won experience in the Battle of the Atlantic to produce new classes of anti-submarine frigates in the 1950s Typical of these is HMCS *Margaree* which was completed in 1957. A few years later she was modified by the addition of a large hangar flightdeck as shown in this 1966 view. *via L. Marriott*

RIGHT: The Italian helicopter cruiser *Vittorio Veneto* is one of the oldest major warships currently in service. Launched in 1967, she is likely to remain in service until replaced by a new aircraft carrier in 2007. Armament comprises Teseo anti-ship and Standard surface-to-air missiles, as well as an impressive battery of 3-inch automatic guns and up to six Agusta Bell AB212ASW helicopters. *via L. Marriott*

FAR RIGHT: The "Daring" class destroyers, completed in the early 1950s, embodied all the lessons of World War II. They were fast and powerful ships but with a rather ungainly appearance due to the fore-funnel being partly hidden within the lattice foremast. Eight were built for the Royal Navy and a further three for Australia. *via L.Marriott*

Korea

The Korean War (1950-53) arose from the Cold War, as the civil war between the Communist North Koreans and South Korea led to intervention by an Allied UN force of US-led troops assisting South Korea and the Chinese assisting the North Koreans. Possibly the most daring action of the war was General MacArthur's amphibious assault on the enemy's rear at Inchon on September 15, 1950, to relieve pressure on UN forces to the south. Supported by a naval bombardment and F-4U Corsair fighter-bombers of Marine Aircraft Wing 1, the 1st Marine Division made its first attack at dawn. Many of the assault craft dated from World War II and a number even had to be reclaimed from the Japanese. A second successful assault took place later in the day and within two weeks a reinforced UN force had encircled and destroyed the Northern Korean forces in the southern Korean peninsula. As well as supporting amphibious assaults, naval forces were also used during the Korean War to bombard shore positions and carry out blockading patrols up coast (the US Navy concentrating on the east side of Korea, the Royal Navy on the west), supported by carriers, and bringing in supplies and reinforcements to the land-based forces.

armament by a rather ugly flightdeck and hangar. In this form they could operate up four Wessex or Sea King ASW helicopters.

The development of the guided missile was one reason why no more conventional destroyers were completed after the "Darings." The great bulk of the missile, together with its magazine-handling system, required a considerable hull volume and the "County" class destroyers, which entered service from 1963 onward, were, at 5,500 tons displacement, considerably larger than anything which had gone before. Originally armed with four 4.5-inch guns forward, and a single twin Seaslug missile launcher right aft, there were also facilities for the operation of a Wessex helicopter and the upperworks were dominated by the search and tracking radars required to support the missile system. The

ABOVE: **The only new cruisers commissioned by the Royal Navy after World War II were the three "Tiger" class which were finally completed in 1959-61. As conventional cruisers they introduced the automatic 6-inch gun capable of firing 20 rounds per minute.** *via L.Marriott*

LEFT: **HMS *Blake*, one of two "Tiger" class cruisers converted to operate four Wessex ASW helicopters from a substantial hangar and flightdeck structure which replaced the after 6-inch gun mounting.** *via L.Marriott*

OVERLEAF: **In the mid 1970s, most of the County class destroyers were modified to ship the Exocet anti ship missile, one of which is being launched here. This modification entailed the removal of one of the twin 4.5in gun mountings.** *via L.Marriott*

development of the smaller Sea Dart missile resulted in the more compact — many said too compact — all-gas turbine-powered Type 42 of which the name ship, HMS *Sheffield*, commissioned in 1975. This ship was sunk by an Argentine air-launched Exocet missile during the Falklands War, and a sister ship (HMS *Coventry*) fell to a rain of bombs from a flight of A-4 Skyhawks. Nevertheless, other ships of the class, notably HMS *Exeter*, gave a good account of themselves and substantially assisted the air defence of the whole task force. A total of 12 Type 42s was built, including four lengthened Batch II ships.

As a result of the Falklands experience, these latter ships are now fitted with a Vulcan Phalanx Close-in Weapons System (CIWS) for short-range defence against air attack. There are a number of CIWS in use with the world's navies, and they all incorporate their own track and scan radar systems as part of an automatic fire control system. Once an incoming target is detected, it is tracked and the gun opens fire automatically as soon as the a target is within range, typically at 2,000-3,000yds. The very high rate of fire (3,000-4000 rounds per minute) almost guarantees a hit after only a very short burst.

The remaining Type 42s are very long in the tooth, and their replacement has been a high priority fro some time. In 2001 the first of the new Type 45 destroyers were ordered, and the first of these is due to be completed in 2007. These will be armed with the PAAMS (principal anti-air missile system) which utilize Aster 15 or 30 missiles launched from a vertical silo in the foredeck. This design grew out of attempts by Britain, France and Italy to build a common design under the designation "Project Horizon," although Britain withdrew to produce its own design. The Type 45 will be powered by a new integrated Electric Propulsion system which uses gas-turbines to drive alternators producing up to 42mW of power for the electric motors. In common with many modern warships, the Type 45 employs stealth technology intended to make the ship less easy to

FAR LEFT: **Of a similar size and displacement to the British "County" class destroyers, the Dutch "Tromp" class were built in the early 1970s and presented a balanced design. A Terrier medium-range missile launcher is aft, while a Sea Sparrow short-range SAM launcher and a twin 4.7-inch gun mounting are forward. The ship is all-gas-turbine-powered and could embark a Lynx helicopter. Note the weatherproof dome protecting the long-range air search radar.** *L.Marriott*

LEFT: **The catastrophic effect of a hit by a modern anti-ship missile is illustrated by the damage to HMS *Sheffield* after a successful Exocet attack by Argentine forces during the 1982 Falklands War. Although this hit eventually sank the ship, it is sobering to realize that the missiles warhead did not explode and the damage was caused by ballistic impact and the effects of the burning propellant fuel.** *Bison Picture Library*

ABOVE: **As a result of the Falklands experience, the Royal Navy added additional close-range automatic weapons to all of its warships.**
Bison Picture Library

LEFT: **HMS *Edinburgh*, one of four lengthened Batch III Type 42 destroyers. These were 40 feet longer than the earlier versions and this improved seakeeping and habitability. However, the longer hull proved prone to stress and strengthening beams, clearly visible in this recent view, were later added on the sheerline amidships.**
L. Marriott

detect by reducing its radar and infra red profile. This is partly achieved by making as much of the hull and super-structure as smooth as possible, and ensuring that all surfaces are at angles calculated to reflect radar waves away from the radar source.

The US Navy built considerably more destroyers in the postwar era staring with "Forrest Sherman" class from 1955 onward. These were handsome flush-decked twin-funneled ships in the best American destroyer tradition, but were armed with a new semi-automatic 5-inch gun. The basic design was echoed in the 3,350-ton "Charles F. Adams" class, built between 1958 and 1964, but these were the first US destroyers to carry a surface-to-air missile in the form of a single Tartar missile launcher right aft. With an ASROC launcher, ASW torpedoes and two 5-inch/5-cal guns, they were well-balanced ships and a number were also ordered by the then West Germany and Australia.

Contemporary with these destroyers were the slightly larger (4,150 tons) "Coontz" class of 10 destroyers, origi-nally rated as frigates, which had a twin launcher for Terrier SAM on the quarter-deck. In 1975 the first "Spruance" class destroyers joined the fleet, and these were first all-gas-turbine warships in the US Navy. Displacing almost 8,000 tons at full load, they were large ships but, strangely, only carried the Sea Sparrow short-range missile for air defence and were really optimized for the ASW role. Most of the 24 completed have now been updated and included the Tomahawk land-attack cruise missile in their inventory.

The US Navy's current destroyer program centers around the DG51 "Arleigh Burke" class, and over 50 of these will have been completed by the end of 2005. These 9,000-ton ships are built around the Aegis air defence sys-tem which incorporates multi-channel track while scan planar array radars which can cope with multiplele targets. The missile element is provided by SM-2 Standard missiles with a range of up to 70 miles. Propulsion is all-gas-turbine, and the hull has a relatively low length to beam ratio, unlike the more traditional long and lean destroyer shape. A version of the Aegis system has been approved for export and arms the four "Kongou" class destroyers of the Japanese Navy, which are almost identical to the "Arleigh Burke" class, and also to Spain which is currently building

ABOVE RIGHT: **The "Spruance" class destroyers were the first all-gas-turbine-powered major warships in the US Navy. This is USS *Deyo* which was completed in 1980. All ships of this class currently in service are fitted with the Mk 41 vertical launch silo which can be seen on the foredeck immediately abaft the gun mounting.** *via L. Marriott*

RIGHT: **USS *Richard E. Byrd*, a "Charles F. Adams" class destroyer, completed in 1964. This one of the most successful American postwar destroyer types and it was also adopted by the Australian and German navies.**
via L. Marriott

ABOVE: **This view emphasizes the wide beam of the US Navy's "Arleigh Burke" class destroyers.** *via L.Marriott*

LEFT: **USS *Gonzalez*, an "Arleigh Burke" class destroyer, running trials at maximum speed. Note the flat panels of the SPY-1D phased-array radar antenna on either side of the bridge superstructure.** *via L.Marriott*

four "Alvaro de Bazan" class air defense frigates to an indigenous design.

The US Navy had large numbers of cruiser available at the end of World War II, and also subsequently completed two "Worcester" class cruisers armed with 12 automatic guns in six twin mountings, similar in concept to the British "Tiger" class but completed much earlier, in 1948-49. Also designed in the war but not completed until 1948-49 were the three 17,000-ton "Des Moines" class cruisers armed with nine semi-automatic 8-inch guns in three triple turrets. However, the US Navy put considerable effort into the development of a variable surface-to-air missile system and produced the short-range Tartar, medium-range Terrier and the long-range Talos systems in the mid-1950s. The compact Terrier subsequently formed the basis for the current Standard missile introduced initially in the mid-1960s. In an effort to get these to sea, a few "Baltimore" and "Cleveland" class cruisers were modified to carry the new missile systems.

The most dramatic cruiser of the post-war era was the 14,200-ton nuclear-powered *Long Beach* which was

ABOVE: **The German shipbuilding industry has gained considerable success over the past two decades with the MEKO 200 modular frigate design. Using a standard hull with a variety of machinery, armament and equipment options, export sales have been made to many countries including Turkey, Greece, Portugal and Australia. Shown here is Turkish *Yavuz*, one of four completed in 1987-89.** *via L. Marriott*

RIGHT: **Italy has built a series of successful frigate designs in the postwar era. This is a "Maestrale" class frigate built in the 1980s and is armed with a 5-inch gun, two twin 40mm compacts and the indigenous Aspide short-range missile system. A helicopter is also embarked.** *via L. Marriott*

completed in 1961, and was also the first US warship equipped with missiles as the main armament. These included Terrier and Talos SAMs, and later Harpoon SSMs, although two 5-inch guns were also added within a year of commissioning. However, the succeeding "Leahy" class, which was conventionally powered, retained the concept of a guided-missile-armed cruiser and carried twin launchers fore and aft for Standard missiles. The USS *Bainbridge*, built at the same time, was basically similar to the "Leahy" but was nuclear-powered. A similar arrangement was followed with the "Belknap" class completed in the late-1960s, which were similar to the preceding ships except that only one missile launcher was carried, although this could fire both Standard and ASROC missiles. USS *Truxtun* was virtually a nuclear-powered version of the "Belknaps." In the 1970s the six ships of the "Virginia" and "California" classes were commissioned, and these were all nuclear-powered. Displacing almost 10,000 tons, they differed mainly in that, while the "California" class had separate launchers for the Standard MR and ASROC missiles, the "Virginias" had a single launcher capable of firing either missile. All are now decommissioned. In fact, the only warships in the US Navy now classified as cruisers are those of the "Ticonderoga" class Aegis cruisers.

The "Ticonderogas" are based on the "Spruance" destroyer hull, but deploy the Aegis missile system. Some 27 have been built, and while the early ships had a Mk 26 twin-missile launcher, later ships had the Mk 41 Vertical

LEFT: **Since the time of the Korean War in the 1950s, Japan has steadily rebuilt her naval forces and the Japanese Maritime Self-Defense Force is now one of the largest and best-equipped in the world. The *Shimakaze* shown here was one of a pair of large gas-turbine-powered destroyers completed in 1986 and 1988. A substantial armament includes two 5-inch guns, Phalanx close-in weapon systems, Harpoon anti-ship and Standard surface-to-air missiles, ASROC and anti-submarine homing torpedoes.** *via L.Marriott*

Launch System on the foredeck. This is a very versatile system which can be used to launch a variety of missiles including the Standard SM-2 SAM, the ASROC ASW missile and Tomahawk land-attack cruise missile. The Aegis system itself is currently being upgraded so that it can intercept ballistic missiles .

Soviet Russia embarked on a substantial destroyer program in the late 1940s and early 1950s, and this resulted in the handsome "Skory" and "Kotlin" classes, which were heavily armed with conventional weapons although some of the 2,800-ton "Kotlins" were subsequently modified to carry a surface-to-air missile launcher instead of the after twin 5.1-inch gun turret. These were followed in the 1960s by the "Kanin" and "Kildin" classes, which were relatively conventional, but the latter shipped the SS-N-2 "Styx" SSM, which was to gain notoriety in 1967 when one of these missiles fired from an Egyptian fast-attack craft sank the Israeli destroyer *Eilat*, an event which shook the naval world at the time, and alerted it to the potentialities of the anti-ship missile. However, Russia's great achievement in the early 1960s was the introduction of the all-gas-turbine-powered 3,750-ton "Kashin" class missile destroyers. Currently the backbone of the Russian destroyer force are the 6,600-ton "Sovremenny class," which are heavily armed with a variety of missile systems as well as mounting two twin automatic 130mm guns capable of firing 45 rounds per minute. At least two of these have been built for China, which may order more.

While the Western Navies produced few new conventional cruisers after World War II, the Soviet Navy pressed ahead and completed no fewer than 14 16,000-ton "Sverdlov" class cruisers armed with 12 6-inch guns in four triple turrets. At the time these caused some consternation to Western navies, as they were difficult to counter except by carrier aircraft. Some were later modified to carry helicopters or guided missiles, and in either case this necessitated the removal of the after gun turrets. The Russians seemed to delight in the production of large heavily armed warships, and in the early 1960s they introduced the 6,000-ton (full load) "Kynda" class cruisers armed with "Shaddock" anti-ship missiles. These were followed by the "Kresta I" and "Kresta II" classes, in which full-load displacement rose to 7,500 tons and which were armed with a variety of missile systems. Western intelligence initially

LEFT: **The latest Russian destroyers are the "Sovremenny" class which was first introduced in 1988. Noticeable features in this aerial view are the twin automatic 130mm gun mountings fore and aft, and the flightdeck positioned amidships where helicopter operations are less affected by pitching motion of the ship than the more common stern platform. At least two vessels of this type have been sold to China.** *L.Marriott*

ABOVE: **USS *Ticonderoga*, name ship of the class of Aegis missile cruisers which were based on the "Spruance" class destroyer hull and machinery.** *Bison Picture Library*

ABOVE RIGHT: **USS *Long Beach*, a guided-missile cruiser and the world's first nuclear-powered warship, commissioned in 1961. This photo shows the ship in her original configuration with twin Terrier missile launchers forward and a twin Talos installation aft. At one stage the ship was intended to carry up to eight Polaris ballistic missiles, but these were never embarked. The huge square superstructure carries the fixed antenna of the SPS-32 and 33 radars.** *Bison Picture Library*

RIGHT: **The "Leahy" class missile cruiser USS *Dale* was launched in 1962. Originally classified as destroyers, the "Leahy" class were redesignated cruisers in 1975.** *via L. Marriott*

OVERLEAF: **Soviet "Sverdlov" cruiser *Aleksandr Suvorov* (CL-834) during Exercise "Okean."** *TRH Pictures/US Navy*

identified the some of latter as anti-ship cruise missiles, but it was eventually realized that they were SS-N-14 anti-submarine missiles, which clearly defined these ships as ASW vessels despite their relatively large size. The final outcome of this line of development was the 10,000-ton "Kara" class completed from 1973 onward. These were very similar to their immediate predecessors except that they were gas-turbine-powered and carried additional surface-to-air missile systems.

While these Soviet cruisers were undoubtedly large, well-armed and potentially difficult neutralize, there were plans as far back as 1968 to produce something infinitely more powerful. The outcome of these plans were the four massive 24,000-ton "Kirov" class nuclear-powered missile cruisers, which were all completed during the 1980s. These were Russia's only nuclear-powered surface warships, and were also the largest surface combat ships to be built for any navy after the end of World War II. Armament included "Shipwreck" cruise missiles with a range of up to 250 miles, no fewer than four different types of surface-to-air missiles capable of engaging aircraft at ranges in excess of 50 miles, as well as guns and ASW weapons. Only two of these battlecruisers currently remain in service, as the post-Cold War Russian Navy struggles to find the funding to maintain a balanced fleet in commission. Consequently, the smaller 12,000-ton "Slava" class cruisers, built at the same time as the "Kirovs," are more favored and at least three are currently in commission. A conventional gas-turbine machinery system is installed in preference to a nuclear powerplant, but a

LEFT: Russian "Sverdlov" class light cruiser armed with 6-inch guns. These vessels were the only conventional cruisers to be laid down by any nation after World War II. *TRH Pictures*

BELOW: The USS *Albany* was one of three heavy cruisers laid down in 1944, which were eventually completed converted as "double-ended" missile cruisers. They carried twin Talos long-range SAM launchers fore and aft, and Tartar short-range SAM launchers abreast the massive bridge. Note the multitude of search and tracking radars associated with these missile systems. *via L. Marriott*

battery of 16 "Sandbox" 300-mile range cruise missiles are carried, together with short- and long-range surface-to-air missiles, twin 130mm automatic guns, torpedoes, ASW mortars and a helicopter. These two classes of cruiser pack a heavy anti-ship punch and as such, they make up, to a certain extent, for the lack of a carrier force in the Russian Navy.

Apart from carriers, submarines and surface combatants, the other great evolution in the postwar era is the continued development of specialized ships for amphibious warfare. Although the great set-piece invasions of World War II are unlikely to be repeated on such a grand scale, a study of postwar operations shows that amphibious forces have been an integral part of many conflicts. One of the greatest advances was the improvement of the helicopter to the stage where a single machine could transport a worthwhile number of armed troops and subsequently could lift heavy items of equipment including vehicles and artillery. One of the earliest successful application of helicopters in the amphibious assault role occurred during the 1956 Suez

ABOVE: **"Kirov" class nuclear-powered battlecruiser built during the 1980s.** *TRH Pictures*

RIGHT: **A Russian "Kresta II" missile-armed cruiser in the mid-1970s. Like most large Soviet warships, they carried a much more extensive weapon outfit than western ships of a similar displacement. The large missile canisters on either side of the bridge actually house SS-N-14 long-range ASW missiles, indicating that these ships were primarily intended for this role.** *via L.Marriott*

Crisis, when British and French forces attacked and occupied the Suez Canal area. Although a political disaster, the military operation run like clockwork, and included the landing of Royal Marines direct onto Gamil airfield by means of helicopters from the light fleet carriers *Ocean* and *Theseus*. The success of this operation led to the conversion of two more modern carriers to the assault role (HMSs *Albion* and *Bulwark*), and subsequently the fleet carrier *Hermes* was also converted, although the latter was hastily recommissioned to operate fixed-wing Sea Harriers for the Falklands campaign. However, despite the Royal Navy's wholehearted support for the concept of a helicopter assault carrier, it did not commission a purpose-built vessel of this type until 1998 when the 22,000-ton HMS *Ocean* entered service, by which time all of the other assault carriers had long been retired.

The availability of great numbers of wartime landing ships meant that some time was to elapse before new purpose-built ships entered service, but the Suez operation demonstrated that many of these were too old for further service and this led to the building in the 1960s of two

Amphibious Warfare

After the Allies' successful amphibious landings in World War II, many strategists felt that the rise of nuclear weapons obviated the need to maintain an amphibious capacity. However, the success of the Marines' landings at Inchon in the Korean War, and the fact it became obvious that nuclear weapons would not be used in the conflict, vindicated the continued development of amphibious warfare. The biggest change in postwar amphibious warfare has been the introduction of the helicopter, giving a sea-borne assault greater speed and flexibility, the first combat amphibious assault using helicopters being by the British during the Suez Crisis in 1956. The first helicopter carriers (LPHs) were converted aircraft carriers but dedicated helicopter assault ships have subsequently been built, led by the US Navy's *Iwo Jima* which entered service in 1961. The Americans have continued to lead the way in amphibious warfare postwar with the development of the LPD — the amphibious landing dock — which contains its own well dock carrying a number of various landing craft (LCUs, LCMs or LVTs) as well as a flightdeck. This design has been copied by many other navies, including Britain's "Fearless" class, and is extremely effective in conjuction with LPHs. This development has been taken a stage further by the US Navy's "Tarawa" class LHAs, which combine the LPD and LPH in one large assault ship. Other recent developments have included the US Newport class landing craft with a ramp lowered from above the bow of a conventional hull rather than being built with the traditional integral ramp or bow doors which reduce speed, and purpose-built command ships with sophisticated command and communications facilities.

TOP LEFT: **A clear view of a "Kirov" class battlecruiser showing the missile silos on the foredeck.**
TRH Pictures/DoD

LEFT: **HMS *Ocean* is the Royal Navy's latest amphibious warfare asset. Capable of accommodating over 1,000 troops, she can also embark a squadron of 12 Sea King helicopters to deploy them rapidly ashore.** *L. Marriott*

Falklands

The remote position of the Falkland Islands in the South Atlantic meant that naval support was vital in the Falklands War (1982) between Argentina and Britain. Following the Argentine invasion of the islands, Britain dispatched a task force, including the converted cruise liner *Canberra*, in April 1982. When it arrived at the Falklands a total exclusion zone was set up around the islands, and the Royal Navy conducted operations intended both to keep the Argentine Navy within its own coastal waters — including a helicopter attack which seriously damaged the Argentine submarine *Santa Fe* — and also in preparation for a land attack. The sinking of the Argentine cruiser *General Belgrano* on May 2 by the submarine HMS *Conqueror*, actually took place outside the total exclusion zone. On May 21 the ground forces were landed at San Carlos, with the Royal Navy providing air defence, bombarding Argentine shore positions, screening supply convoys and landing and recovering special forces. British troops retook the islands but the Royal Navy suffered a number of casualties while in San Carlos Water — the destroyer HMS *Sheffield* was sunk by an air-launched AM.39 Exocet missile, the frigates HMS *Ardent* and HMS *Antelope*, and the merchantman *Atlantic Conveyor*, were also all sunk by Argentine Navy aircraft. Several other ships were hit and the Royal Fleet Auxiliary LSL (Landing Ships Logistics) Sir *Galahad* was also so badly damaged she had to be scuttled.

assault ships, *Fearless* and *Intrepid*, otherwise known as Landing Ships (Dock) — LPD. These followed the idea, first applied in World War II, of having a ship large enough to carry troops and armored vehicles, together with the necessary landing craft, in a floodable well or dock at the stern. The integration of all these elements in one ship was an advance on previous practice, and a further step forward was the provision of a large flightdeck which could accommodate several helicopters, although there were no hangar facilities. These two ships had a varied and arduous career and are now laid up, with two modern replacements due in 2003.

As might be expected, American efforts in this field were on a much grander scale than the British. While the Royal Navy experimented with helicopters, the US Navy converted one of the wartime escort carriers for trials

*LEFT: **Kirov** on trials in the Baltic. The class has formidable AAA armament including SA-N6 and SA-N3 missiles, also SA-N4 launchers and 30mm guns. TRH Pictures/Royal Navy*

purposes, but followed up in the 1960s with seven purpose-built 11,000-ton "Iwo Jima" class assault carriers designed to carry a Marine battalion and all their equipment, and land them by means of helicopters. A number of "Essex" class fleet carriers were also converted for the amphibious warfare role. In the 1970s the much larger "Tarawa" class were produced, and at 40,000 tons full load they were equal in size to many conventional aircraft carriers. However, they differed from previous assault carriers in that they also incorporated a stern dock which could accommodate a variety of landing craft, including LCAC air-cushion vehicles (hovercraft) so that up to 1,700 troops and all their vehicles, stores and equipment could be transported and landed by sea and air lift. A progressive development of the "Tarawa" design is the current "Wasp" class, which is very similar but can accommodate almost 2,000 troops and presents a slightly different profile, with a lowered bridge and superstructure. Both classes can operate AV-8B Harriers for close-air support if required.

The US Navy has also built substantial numbers of dock landing ships and amphibious transports from the late 1950s onward, and has also built a number of specialized command ships. For the future, the backbone of amphibious operations, apart from the assault carriers, will be the new LPD-17 class, the first of which due to commission in 2003. Each will carry a 750-strong Marine combat group which will be landed by a combination of heavy lift helicopters and LCACs. Central to US Navy amphibious strategy is the new V-22 Osprey tilt rotor tactical transport which will be capable of carrying up to 24 troops at speeds up to 350 knots, substantially faster than any helicopter. This will operate from both the assault carriers and LPDs when it enters operational service in a few years time.

As the world's navies enter the 21st century, the shape of things to come is growing clearer. Individual ships will rely heavily on automated and computer-assisted systems in order to operate efficiently and also to reduce manning requirements. The outline of many ships is undergoing a substantial change, as more and more incorporate stealth technology to make themselves less visible to a whole spectrum of sensors. Pioneered by the French "La Fayette" class frigates, the stealth look hides much of a warships weaponry and equipment behind flat-angled sides. Another trend is for vertical-launch silos to replace trainable launchers, particularly as these can be easily adapted to handle virtually any sort of missile, so that a warship only needs one multi-cell silo to handle anti-aircraft, anti-ship and anti-submarine missiles, as well as long-range land-attack cruise missiles. The ultimate expression of this concept was the so-called arsenal ship considered recently by the US Navy. This would have been a very large vessel with a simple stealth profile and would have stood offshore in naval operations, ready to saturate the area with numerous missiles of all types. Although abandoned, many of the concepts will

Helicopters and Ships

The earliest experiments with rotary wing aircraft taking-off from warships took place in the 1930s, leading to the first limited use of helicopters by the Germans and Americans during World War II. Postwar developments, particularly by the USA, USSR and Britain, used helicopters largely in non-combat roles such as communications, rescue or observation although their power and carrying capacity had developed sufficiently by the time the first helicopter assault took place from Royal Navy carriers during the Suez Crisis in 1956. Today's naval helicopters are used in a wide range of roles, particularly ASW, but also ASST (anti-ship surveillance and targeting), AEW (airborne early warning), troop carrying and commando-style assault. The most widely used helicopters today include smaller aircraft such as the Westland Lynx developed for the Royal Navy and the French Navy, and larger aircraft such as the US Navy's Sikorsky SH-60B Seahawk and its latest variant, the SH-60F, the Sikorsky/Westland Sea King and its replacement the Agusta-Westland EH-101 Merlin, all of which can carry the latest ASW, AEW and anti-ship guided missiles and anti-submarine torpedoes, and can be carried on most warships from large aircraft carriers to small frigates. French, Russian and Italian manufacturers such as Aerospatiale, Agusta-Bell and Kamov have also developed other helicopters which have been sold around the world.

be applied to the new DD21 land-attack destroyer to be in service from 2010 onward.

In Europe, most major navies are embarking on the production of sophisticated air defence destroyers with an attack capability. These included the British Type 45, the Dutch "de Zeven Provicien" and Spanish "F100." No more ballistic missile submarines are likely to be built, but most large submarines can now carry sub-launched cruise missiles which can carry nuclear warheads to ranges of over 1,000 miles. While the US Navy continues with the building of super-carriers, the smaller navies, including Britain, are looking at new ships which will operate the new internationally developed Joint Strike Fighter (JSF) which will be available in either conventional or vertical take-off forms. While guided missiles now form the main armament of most warships, the naval gun is actually undergoing something of a renaissance with the concept of extended-

LEFT: **The shape of things to come? The Royal Navy has already commissioned a trimaran research vessel (*Triton*) and this is an artist's impression of a warship based on this concept. Advantages of this configuration include improved stability and a much greater deck area for installing weapons and equipment.** *via L .Marriott*

BELOW LEFT: **The increasing sophistication of modern warships has made them extremely expensive to design and build. In an effort to reduce and share costs, several international programs have been attempted in recent years. One major project was the NATO Frigate concept of the early 1990s, shown here in model form. However, this was cancelled and the subsequent multinational Project Horizon frigate will now only be built by France and Italy, other countries originally involved such as Spain, United Kingdom and the Netherlands have opted for national programs.** *via L. Marriott*

BELOW: **"La Fayette" class frigate *Courbet* under way. This view emphasizes the clean lines of the ships which are quite lightly armed with little ASW potential.** *via L. Marriott*

BELOW: HMS *Albion*, one of two aircraft carriers converted to the amphibious assault role at the start of 1960s and built on experience gained in the ill-fated Anglo-French Suez operation. *via L. Marriott*

range guided munitions which will make them capable of very accurate fire at ranges of over 70 miles.

At one time in the postwar period, it was thought in some quarters that the day of the warship was coming to an end in the face of atomic weapons and air power. Today it can be seen that nothing is further from the truth and that, as long was we live in troubled world, there will always be a role for naval forces. The acceptance of that role will demand warships of the highest quality capable of providing offensive power and support when required, but also capable of defending themselves against the most sophisticated attacks. Such quality does not come cheaply but, then, peace and freedom never did.

LEFT: **The assault ship HMS *Fearless*, completed in 1967. This specialized vessel could transport several hundred troops and put them ashore, with their vehicles and equipment, by means of landing craft and helicopters. The entrance to the stern dock which accommodated four Tank Landing Craft (LCT) can just be seen in this view of the ship on exercise off the Norwegian coast.** *via L. Marriott*

BELOW: Kirov **on sea trials.** *TRH Pictures/US Navy*

Electronic Warfare

Electronic systems, including stealth technology, have the capacity to take over many of the defensive functions carried out by warships. Although much secrecy surrounds the details of each navy's electronic warfare (EW) equipment, in general modern ship-based EW has both an ESM (electronic support measures), or detection, capacity and a ECM (electronic countermeasures), or jamming, capacity. The common system installed on US ships is the SLQ-32(V)2/3 EW system, and similar systems are used by a number of other navies including the French ARBR 17/ARBB 33 and the British RAPIDS/SCIMITAR, as well as the Russian fleet although details are not known of its system. These systems consist of a radar search receiver using a multi-port or rotating dish aerial, which assesses the electronic emissions, identifying and classifying the information to detect ships and aircraft or an attack from beyond the horizon, and, if necessary, passes the information on to other ships in the force. The ECM component is linked to the radar and, if there is a threat ,reacts directly to the ESM surveillance, as well as having the capacity to respond to command instructions. The "jammer" searches its library for a target matching the characteristics input, and when the target is identified locks on to it by frequency and direction, causing confusion to the target radar by creating echoes with false ranges and bearings which incoming missiles will follow rather than locking on to the warship.

Stealth Ships

Stealth ships were first seriously used in World War I when ships would have their appearance disguised by camouflage or a false superstructure. The rise of electronic technology, such as sonar and radar, has meant that the disguise has had to become equally sophisticated electronically. The latest class of US Navy destroyers, the "Arleigh Burke" class, has been fitted with the latest range of stealth technology features that have been tested by a "stealth ship," the USS *Sea Shadow*. This experimental vessel has been designed specifically to test new stealth technologies, its angular design providing a low radar profile so as to render it nearly invisible to electronic surveillance. The latest French frigates in the "La Fayette" class are also among the most advanced warships using stealth technology, their entire structure being designed with stealth in mind. This technology includes masking propeller noise by passing air bubbles around the hull, using radar absorbent material (RAM) to disguise the vessel's radar profile and funnel baffles to disperse exhaust gases and make the ship less vulnerable to infra-red detection. A range of stealth technologies have also been developed specifically for submarines, including coating their hulls in anechoic tiles which absorb sonar transmissions as well as various systems to reduce propeller noise, such as shrouding the propeller and driving it with a pump-jet.

RIGHT: **An impression of a new 3,700-ton frigate to be built for the Norwegian Navy by the Spanish shipbuilders, Bazan. The design embraces features found on many modern warships including stealth outline, a vertical-launch missile silo and a range of electro-optical sensors.** *via L. Marriott*

BELOW: **The French Navy has pioneered the stealth frigate with its "La Fayette" class, which began entering service from 1996. The clean angled hull and superstructure surfaces are designed to reduce radar reflections so that they are more difficult to detect. Most future designs, such as the British Type 45 destroyer, will adopt a similar technique.** *L. Marriott*

Index